Apartheid:
The Story of
a Dispossessed People

Motsoko Pheko

Marram Books
101 Kilburn Square, London NW6 6PS

Apartheid—The Story of a Dispossessed People
was first published in 1972 by
Sharpville Day Association, Dar-Es-Salaam,

Second revised edition in 1984 by Marram Books
101 Kilburn Square, London NW6 6PS

Cover designed by Len Breen
Set by Grassroots, London.
Printed by Whitstable Litho Ltd., Whitstable, Kent

British Library Cataloguing in Publication Data
Pheko, Motsoko.
    Apartheid—2nd edition
    1. Blacks—South Africa—Segregation—
    History   2. South Africa—Race Relations
    I. Title
    323.1'68   DT763

ISBN 0-906334-04-7

Contents

Diary of Some Historical Events in Azania

460 A.D.	Africans occupy Azania (some historians point to a much earlier date '...the early stages of the evolutionary cycle,' they say).
950	Black Iron Age People are established at Palaboroa.
1025	Iron Age civilisation in the Witwatersrand area (Ga Ramogale).
1400	Black Iron Age People are established at Mapungubwe, centre of a great Azanian civilisation.
1450	A Mofokeng King marries a San woman for his senior wife. This leads to the split of the kingdom when he dies.
1487	Bartholomew Diaz reaches 'the Cape of Storms' in Azania.
1497	Vasco da Gama lands in Zululand on Christmas Day and renames this part of Azania, Natal (Land of Nativity in commemoration of Christ's birthday).
1503	Antonia de Salha sails to Table Bay.
1509	Don Francisco de Almeida sails from Malbar in Asia to Azania.
1510	The first war and battle between the Khoi Africans in Azania and the Portuguese invaders, and the Africans are victorious.
1552	One of the largest Portuguese ships called Saint John is wrecked by a fierce storm as it nears Umtamvuna in the Cape.
1554	Saint Benedict ship is wrecked in the area of Mbashe River.
1580	Francis Drake and his crew sail to Azania.
1591	Three English ships sail out of Plymouth under the command of Admiral George Raymond heading for Azania.
1593	A Portuguese ship Saint Alberto is wrecked south of Umtata River.
1602	The Dutch East India Company is formed in Holland.
1604	The Dutch East India Company grabs Bantam and Java which had rich spices in Asia.
1641	The first African to learn English, Xhore or Quore returns from England.
1647	A Dutch ship called Haarlem is wrecked in Table Bay. Its survivors were Nicholaas Proot and Leender Janssen.
1652	Jan van Riebeeck, an official of the Dutch East India Company establishes a 'provision station' near today's Capetown.
1652	Chief Qora of the Khoi Africans is killed resisting Dutch colonial invasion and settlement in Azania.
1653	The officials of the Dutch East India Company accuse the Khoi Africans of 'stealing' their cattle.
1654	Jan van Riebeeck discourages 'private trade' between the Khoi and

the individual workers of the Dutch East India Company.

1657	Jan van Riebeeck sends out his men to persuade the Khoi Africans living in the interior to sell cattle to the Dutch East India Company.
1667	The Khoi Africans fight their third war against the colonial settlers.
1685	Jan van Riebeeck begins to know the difference between the Khoi and the San people.
1687	The Khoi Africans are completely crushed by the colonialists.
1687	A vessel called Noord is sent by the Dutch East India Company to search for survivors of wrecked ships.
1689	Simon van der Stel, a settler governor replaces Jan van Riebeeck.
1715	Smallpox is introduced into the Cape settlement from a passing ship from Europe. The disease kills thousands of Khoi people.
1770	War between the San Africans and the colonial invaders breaks out.
1772	Many San people are killed by Dutch colonialists and are taken prisoners. The San prisoners not being used to prison conditions die in great numbers.
1774	Baron Joachim van Plettenberg in Holland instructs colonial governor Gothfreid Opperman to destroy the San people.
1779-1781	First Xhosa War on record resisting colonialism.
1793	Second Xhosa War of national resistance.
1795	The Cape comes under British colonial rule.
1799-1802	Third Xhosa War of Resistance.
1811-12	Fourth Xhosa War of national resistance against colonialism.
1818-19	Fifth Xhosa War against colonialism.
1830	King Dingane tries unsuccessfully to establish diplomatic relations with the King of England. His aim was to get his army equipped with guns.
1834-35	Sixth Xhosa War against colonialism.
1836	Mzilikazi enters into a Treaty of Agreement with a British colonial governor at the Cape Colony. But he did not intervene when the Boers attacked Mzilikazi.
1836	The Boer invaders arriving in today's Transvaal attack Mzilikazi and the Battle of Vegkop is fought.
1837	the Boer aggressors attack Mzilikazi again in a surprise attack and he flees with his Ndebele people to southern Zimbabwe.
1838	The Battle of Blood River is fought with Mpande on the enemy's side.
1839	King Dingane flees his country and is said to have been killed by 'hostile tribes'.
1846	The British colonial government attacks the Xhosa Africans under King Sandile.
1850	The Khoi join the Xhosa Africans in battle against the British colonial government and they together score victory after victory against the colonial troops of the British.
1850-53	The 11th and most fiercest Xhosa War against colonial settlers is fought.
1851	King Moshoeshoe defies the British colonial government under

	Warden over a boundary dispute. The Battle of Viervoet is fought and the Basotho Africans defeat the colonial army.
1852	The British Government recognises the 'republic' of the Boer settlers in the Transvaal by signing the Treaty of Sand River.
1852	George Cathcart, a British colonial governor gives King Moshoeshoe an ultimatum to return the 'stolen' cattle.
1854	The Orange Free State 'republic' under the Boers by force of arms is recognised by the British Government by signing the Bloemfontein Convention.
1858	The First Basuto War with the Boer settlers over African land they are grabbing.
1862	A Griqua (Khoi African) chief, Cornelius Waterboer claims land along the Vaal and Harts rivers (Campbell Lands) grabbed from him by the settlers.
1865	Moshoeshoe orders his people to occupy Winburg and Harrismith taken from them by the Boer settlers by virtue of the unscrupulous Warden Line.
1865	Makoanyane, a great Mosotho African warrior kills the Boer commander, Wepner at the Battle of Thaba Bosiu.
1865	The Second Basuto War and a combined army of the Free State and Transvaal Boers is defeated.
1867-69	The Third Basuto War of Resistance against the Boers.
1876	The Bapedi Africans defeat the Boers and the British intervene on the side of the Boer settlers and aggressors.
1877	The British annex the Transvaal.
1879	The Battle of Isandlwana where the Zulu Africans defeat the British army ignominiously.
1882	Imbumba YamaAfrika is formed in eastern Cape Colony.
1884	The Native Education Association is formed.
1884	Rev Nehemiah Tile forms the Independent Tembu Church as a protest against racial discrimination in the church.
1884	The Native Electoral Association is formed in Kingwilliamstown.
1892	Rev Mangena founds the Ethiopian Church in Pretoria.
1898	The Ethiopian Church joins the African Methodist Episcopal Church in the USA.
1902	The British Government repeals the Sand River and Bloemfontein Conventions and annexes the Transvaal and the Orange Free State making them 'British possessions'.
1902	South African Native Congress is formed in eastern Cape Colony.
1902	African Political (later Peoples') Organization is formed in Capetown by Dr Abdullah Abdurahman.
1903	South African Races Congress is formed in the Cape.
1904	Natal Native Congress is formed.
1905	Native United Political Association of the Transvaal is formed.
1906	The Orange River Colony Native Congress is formed.
1908	The settlers hold a 'national convention' in Durban and exclude Africans.

1909	The British Parliament passes the Union of South Africa Act making the African country 'independent and sovereign' under the Anglo-Boer settlers.
1910	349,837 settlers in the Cape Colony, Natal, Transvaal and Free State form a Union of South Africa and excludes 5,000,000 indigenous Africans.
1912	African National Congress is formed.
1919	The first African trade union called the Industrial and Commercial Union is formed under the leadership of Clements Kadalie.
1921	The white middle class of South Africa forms the South African Communist Party.
1922	The Rand Miners' Strike is organised by white workers led by the Communist Party of South Africa. They display racist slogans such as 'Workers of the World Unite to fight for a white South Africa!'.
1928	The Independent Black Republic Thesis of 1928 by the Executive Committee of the Communist International at the Sixth World Congress is opposed by the South African Communist Party.
1930	The Independent African National Congress is formed in the Western Cape by Bransby Ndobe and Elliot Tonjeni. It supported the Independent Black Republic Thesis of the Comintern.
1935	The All African Convention is formed to fight the 'Hertzog's Bill'.
1937	A Native Representative Council is legislated by the settler government to 'represent' Africans in Parliament.
1943	The Non-European Unity Movement is formed with I.B. Tabata as one of its leaders.
1944	The Congress Youth Leage is formed which later forms the nucleus of the Pan Africanist Congress.
1949	The militancy urged by the Congress Youth League leads to the adoption of the 1949 Programme of Action.
1950	The South African Communist Party dissolves itself.
1952	The 1949 Programme of Action results in the defiance campaing by the ANC.
1954	South African Congress of Trades Union is formed.
1955	The South African Communist Party sabotages the 1949 Programme of Action and comes up with the Freedom Charter. This splits the Azanian liberation movement.
1956	Clothing Workers Union is formed.
1958	The Africanists leave the ANC.
1959	The Pan Africanist Congress is formed with Mangaliso Robert Sobukwe as its first President.
1959	Federation of Free African Trade Unions of South Africa (FOFATUSA) with J.D. Nyaose as its Secretary-General.
1960	The Pan Africanist Congress launches the historic positive action campaign against the Pass Laws which results in the 'Sharpeville' shootings by the settler police in which 84 people are killed and 365 seriously wounded.
1960	For the first time in the history of South Africa, the settler

	government declares the state of emergency to contain the Pan Africanist Congress and subsequently bans the one-year old PAC and also the then 48 year old ANC.
1960	As a result of the PAC campaign against the Pass Laws, the passes are suspended.
1960	Mangaliso Sobukwe is sentenced to three years imprisonment for inciting Africans to defy Pass Laws with a view to having them abolished.
1962	POQO the military wing of the PAC fights the Battle of Paarl and several policemen are killed.
1963	The Snyman Commission reveals that PAC and POQO are one and the same thing and that PAC is planning another uprising.
1963	Six activists and leaders of the Pan Africanist Congress are sentenced to life imprisonment.
1963	The 'Sobukwe Clause' is made specially to detain Mangaliso Sobukwe, the PAC President. He is not released from jail on completion of his sentence, but is sent to Robben Island where thousands of PAC prisoners are also imprisoned for the POQO Uprising'.
1964	ANC leaders including Nelson Mandela are sentenced to life imprisonment.
1966	John Pokela a PAC leader is kidnapped from Lesotho by the South African police. He is tried and sentenced to 20 years imprisonment on two political charges.
1966	Leaders of the South African Coloured Peoples Congress dissolve their Congress and join the Pan Africanist Congress.
1967	ANC guerrillas fight in Rhodesia with ZAPU in a newly formed military alliance signed by James Chikerema of ZAPU and Oliver Tambo of the ANC.
1968	PAC guerrillas clash with Portuguese soldiers in colonial Mozambique on their way home from military training abroad. They inflict heavy casualties on Portuguese soldiers resulting in South Africa organising 'Operation Sibasa'.
1968	South African Students Organisation (SASO) is formed.
1972	The Black People's Convention is formed with Steve Biko as its Honorary President.
1972	The Black Allied Workers Union is formed with Drake Koka as its Secretary-General.
1973	The African Food and Canning Workers Union (AFCWU) is formed.
1974	SASO and BPC organise 'the FRELIMO Rally' to express solidarity with the people of Mozambique.
1976	The Soweto Uprising in which over 1000 children are killed by the settler police and soldiers explodes into the international scene. It is led by the Black Consciousness Movement of Azania and the Pan Africanist Congress is also implicated.
1977	Steve Biko dies in police custody.
1977	The Black Consciousness Movement representing 18 African political organisations is banned.

1977   The Azanian Peoples Organisation is formed.

1978   Mangaliso Robert Sobukwe dies in restriction in Kimberley still a banned person. Settler government says the cause is cancer, but his PAC colleagues say he was poisoned while on Robben Island.

1978   The Azanian Students Organisation (AZASO) is formed.

1979   Zephania L. Mothopeng is sentenced to 30 years imprisonment for PAC 'terrorist activities' in a case described as 'South Africa's biggest trial, and the longest in the country's judicial history.' The trial was heard in camera.

1979   South African Youth Revolutionary Council is formed with Khotso Seatlholo as its leader. He was later arrested and charged with receiving military training abroad and for other 'terrorist activities' and is sentenced to 25 years imprisonment.

1979   Federation of South African Trade Union (FOSATU) is formed.

1979   South African Allied Workers Union (SAAWU) is formed with Sam Kikine as Secretary-General.

1980   Azania National Youth Union is formed.

1983   Mine Workers Union is formed with Cyril Ramaphosa as Secretary-General.

1983   Azanian Students Movement is formed because AZASO has defected to the 'Freedom' Charter.

1983   United Democratic Front is formed and supports the Freedom Charter.

1983   The National Forum Committee is formed and it issues The Azanian Peoples Manifesto.

Foreword

This book is one of the most remarkable history books that I have read for many years. I know that that sentence will have been misread. I am not speaking about remarkable history books on Africa or about remarkable history books by an African—I am speaking about history books in general. I believe my primary duty is to say why this book occupies such a place in my conception and constant attention to books on history in general and on Africa in particular.

Most history books on Africa are written from a Western historical point of view. I remember going to Africa many times to universities to speak on Africa and doing so to the satisfaction of my audience. But some years ago I spoke on Africa in the United States to a small audience. It went very well until I came to the conclusion when I outlined the future of Africa as not developing from its own powers, but along the lines of Western civilization. A black man sitting at the back of the small hall, a quiet man wearing a beard, stood up and said that he had listened with great interest to what I had to say until at the end I had placed Africa as seeking to participate in the levels at which the great areas of western civilization aimed.

He had intervened because that was a mistake that he had heard often, and he thought it correct to let me know that that was not the aim of the African people today. He said to the African people today, the European intervention, their mastery of much of Africa and their imposition through the universities and books of the ideas of western civilization—all these things were true but they were merely *episodes* in the history of Africa. A time was coming, the time had begun already, when Africa would throw that, all that, off: people would remember it only as history because the African people would then begin to develop and expand in accordance with the nature of the country, with its history and the future to which that environment in Africa and the history of Africa directed them. To associate them always as if aspiring to make their future with the people of western

Europe was a fundamental mistake.

I must say I was startled. I had known that the future of Africa was not going to be an imitation of western civilization. But that it had such a strong, independent view of its own development and looked upon the whole Western intervention in Africa as merely an episode in the history of the great continent—that was something new to me.

I began to re-read and to study, and to try to develop in my own thinking these ideas. I saw many things that I had not seen before. I remember reading a debate on African philosophy in which there was one school which said that the African students of philosophy merely gathered information of the local African territories and handed them to European philosophers who incorporated them into the history of philosophy. An opposition went very far. They said that until these students of philosophy began to write in the native African languages and could be read and understood, and communication begun with the native African people, their philosophy would not have any real value. To write an African philosophy they had to write it in Africa, in an African language and in relation to an African people. That went further in the ideas that the intervention in my lecture had given me.

And now I come to this book and here for the first time is a man writing the history mainly of South Africa. The book from beginning to end deals with the South African struggle—the beginnings from early times, what was the origin of civilization in Southern Africa in general and then the intervenion of the people of the West and the struggles against them. All through reading it I am aware that this is a new history. He is writing the history of Africa, of Southern Africa. He is, I believe, a Southern African himself, grew up in Southern Africa, he may have been educated abroad but that does not matter—he now sees himself as a part of the Southern Africa revolutionary movement dealing with the history of South Africa in a Southern African way.

I do not think I have anything more to say about the book. I have thought that the first thing to do is to make it clear what kind of a book it is—it is a most unusual and most valuable, and in fact, a most precious book.

I have to add one statement. Everybody who talks about Africa in any informed way knows that the West Indians played a great role, within the last two or three generations, in drawing attention to the history of Africa. I believe also that Nkrumah, by achieving the independence that he did in Gold Coast, struck a tremendous blow all over the world for the idea of the independence of Africa. But even if those were incorporated in this history, as I believe they ought to have been done, they would occupy a small place and this book will remain a standard version of the kind of African history that is needed. There may be other books of this kind. If so I should be glad to hear of them.

C.L.R. James
Professor of History
27 February 1984

1. The Falsified History

Racism, separate development and 'freedom', Bantu Homelands, 'whites only', native pass laws, racial discrimination and fascist minority settler rule over the indigenous African majority.

That is apartheid on the surface, but the root of apartheid is the story of a dispossessed people. The story of a stolen land, of bloodshed, colonialism and invasion. The story of indigenous African governments overthrown, and white rule enforced by guns.

South Africa is a blackman's country. It was once ruled by indigenous Africans: it was free and independent. The arrival of Jan van Riebeeck on the 6 April 1652, started the dispossession of the African people. The history of South Africa which followed is a tragic story of military suppression, political oppression, economic exploitation and social degradation of a people, unprecedented in the history of the civilized world. In fact, the contradictions that are found in this history bear a clear stamp of the conflicting interests of the indigenous African majority and those of the settler minority. For over three hundred years the history of what is in reality the story of a dispossessed people, has been falsified in favour of the settlers and their supporters whose writers recorded it in the interest of what they have misnamed 'Western Christian Civilization.'

For instance, in 1959 Eric Louw then Foreign Affairs Minister in the South African apartheid government said, ' ...the Bantu (meaning the African people) began to trek from the North across the Limpopo when Jan van Riebeeck landed in Table Bay in 1652'. He did not explain this coincidence of events. In 1961 Dr Hendrick Verwoerd (Prime Minister assassinated in parliament in September 1966) told a London audience that:

> More than three hundred years ago two population groups
> equally foreign to South Africa converged in rather small

numbers on what was practically empty country. Neither group colonized the other's country or robbed him by invasion.

Dr Verwoerd was born in Holland and went to South Africa with his parents at the age of four, in 1905. It is difficult to know where this Hollander got his information about the history of South Africa.

Of course, many European politicians and writers have characterized this country as roaming wild animals when Jan van Riebeeck built a refreshment station for the Dutch East India Company in 1652. In their bid to 'prove' that they occupied an 'empty land' they have even ignored the fact that Jan van Riebeeck was not the first white man to land in South Africa. They have also closed their eyes to the fact that in 1652 Jan van Riebeeck had no instructions to occupy even Capetown! The Dutch East India Company had no intention of colonizing this part of Africa.

Commenting on the occupation of the Cape, A.H. Keane says,

It is to be noted carefully that the Cape, left almost to itself for over 150 years after its discovery by the Portuguese (1487), was not at first occupied by the Dutch East India Company with a view to colonization. A few seafarers had landed from time to time, in 1520 the English had even taken formal possession in the name of James I, without however, taking any serious steps to settle in the district.[1]

A number of white historians have ignored the fact that Jan van Riebeeck did not occupy the Cape in 1652, but landed on it to build a 'provision station'. Even by European legal and colonial standards there is a difference between landing on a foreign soil and taking occupation of that soil. Of course, the Dutch East India Company provision station later proved to be an effective base from which the Black people of Azania were dispossessed of their country.

The strangest thing, of course, about the history of South Africa is that almost all white historians have tried to make Azania an 'empty land' before it was colonized. In some cases they have even suggested that the Africans were intruders in South Africa. Perhaps this helps to justify apartheid and the national dispossession of the African people by Jan van Riebeeck's descendants, the Voortrekkers.

For instance, J.A. Williamson who wrote *The British Empire and Commonwealth* says:

Far to the eastward, in the better country beyond the Karoo, the frontier Boers were in contact with natives of a different type. These were the Bantu or Kaffirs, a vigorous people with strong tribal organization, military instincts and power of acting in combination, a much more formidable enemy than the Hottentots or the Bushmen. The Kaffirs had worked gradually southwards from the tropical zone and, strictly speaking, were intruders in South Africa just as the white men.[2]

Williamson continues:

The nearest Kaffir tribes to the eastern border of the colony were the Fingos, Pondos and Xhosa. North-east of them, in Natal, dwelt fighting Zulus. North-east of the colony also were also the Basutos, and beyond them, what is now the Transvaal, the Matebele. All these tribes could turn out military forces, and the last three mentioned had a discipline and organization remarkable among Africans. It was fortunate that as yet they had a few firearms or horses, and that their only missile weapon was the assegai or throwing spear.[3]

According to traditional knowledge of their country's history, Africans say that their forefathers occupied South Africa many many centuries before the whiteman set foot on their land. Several old people interviewed from time to time in the past have summed up their views as follows:

Ngumthetho wa Belungu. Bathanda ukuguqul' izinto, NemiBhalo baya ijika xa beqonde ukuba. ABelungu ngomafiki izolo kwelilizwe. Obawo mkhulu bathi kudala babephila naMalawo naBathwa. Amaxhwele amanye amakhulu akwaXhosa kwakungaMalawo. Obawo mkhulu balwe naBelungu, kodwa ke imikhonto yayingasoze imelane nemipu yaBelungu.

That is the habit of the Europeans. They like to twist things to suit them. They never hesitate to change the Scriptures if by that they would get away with some wicked deed. It is not very long since the Europeans came to this country. Our forefathers told us that long ago they lived in this country together with the Khoi and San people (Hottentots and Bushmen). Some of the great traditional doctors among the Xhosas were Khoi. Our forefathers fought to defend this country but were defeated. Assegais were powerless against the might of the European guns.

Other Africans have simply said:

Kajeno re ea lapa ngoan'a ka. Ha re na masimo Makhooa a ne a re nkele lefats'e. Bo ntate-moholo ba ne ba loane senna empa ka ha re ne re loana ka marumo le likoto, Makhooa a loana ka lithunya ba ne ba hlolehe 'me naha ea hapuoa. Ke 'nete hore khale baholo ba rona ba ne ba phela le Baroa le Bakhothu. Ho nyalloana.

Today we starve my child. We have not enough land to produce food and rear cattle. The Europeans took our land from us. Our forefathers fought with assegais and knob-kerries, but Europeans had guns so they took our land. It is true that many years ago our forebears lived side by side with the Khoi and San people. Intermarriage was very common among them.

Many archaeologists have shown that the Iron Age people of the Transvaal in South Africa were established in Palaborwa in the ninth century and at Mapungubwe, the centre of the earlier civilization very similar to the Zimbabwe civilization.

And Leonard Thompson in his contribution to *African Societies in Southern Africa*, writes:

However, we do know that along the Limpopo valley and the Soutpansberg there were in the first half of the second millennium, communities whose material culture was associated with that of contemporaneous Rhodesians iron-working and food producing populations, about whom much more is known at Bambadyanalo in about the 11th century, at Mapungubwe in about the 15th century and at Palaborwa from perhaps the 9th century onwards.[4]

Archaeologists have proved conclusively that the Black people lived in what is now called South Africa as long ago as 460 A.D. Addressing a symposium on ancient mining in October 1973, Professor Revil Mason head of the archaeology department at the University of Witwatersrand, said that 'the early iron age African entered the Transvaal between 1,500 and 2,000 years ago.'

But of course, Azanians occupied this territory long before 460 A.D. James H. Evans of the Faculty of Colgate Rochester Divinity School was right when he wrote:

White South Africans have perpetuated the *myth* that the history of South Africa begins in 1652, the year the Dutch East India

Company established a station at the Cape Peninsula for its crews. According to the myth the land was empty when the white settlers arrived and it was only after their arrival that the African peoples began to move into the region. This is the myth.

The reality, however, is that African peoples were farmers and herdsmen in Southern Africa as early as the third century A.D. Further scientific evidence supports the conclusion that African people have lived in the region since the early stages of the evolutionary cycle.

'Why does the white myth of South Africa differ so widely from the black reality?' The answer to this question in part, he continued 'is that the white invaders found it necessary to justify, historically, their conquest of a large portion of a black continent. By controlling the history of the region, they could control its black inhabitants. Today, a white minority in South Africa sits atop of a despotic political and military regime, the sole aim of which is to keep the black majority in slavery.'[5]

Reaction of Modern Africans to Settler History

The modern generation of Africans has of course, become suspicious of not only the statements made by people like Louw, Verwoerd, white historians and other apartheid settler spokesmen, but of the history of South Africa in general. They suspect that the history of South Africa is written to suit the Europeans and to justify the national dispossession of the Africans and the policy of apartheid.

One such suspicion has been voiced by an African historian and archaeologist. He wrote:

White settlers always try to remove honour conferred upon Africans by antiquity. When they (Europeans) came across the Zimbabwe Ruins for the first time, they credited the famous walls to the Phoenicians, Arabs, Sabaeans etc. With more and more archaeological discoveries being made, however, it has now been proved beyond doubt that the Iron Age Black people of Zimbabwe built the Zimbabwe Walls...

There is also the case of a painting known as 'White Lady of Brandberg' in South West Africa (Namibia). The make up of the lady in the painting is Egyptian. Field Marshal Smuts assisted Abbe Bruil to investigate who was responsible for the

painting. The South African settler government was interested
in the painting because they hoped it might show that Europeans occupied South Africa during the first century of the
Christian era. They failed to prove this ridiculous theory. But
as usual in 1947 the verdict by Abbe Bruil was that the Cretans
or Phoenecians were responsible for the painting.[6]

It seems, however, that there is no intelligent African in Azania who
does not know that the land of his forefathers was usurped and the indigenous Africans dispossessed by the guns of the Europeans. On the
occasion of Heroes' Day July 1959, a national leader (for whom the
apartheid rulers later made a special law called 'Sobukwe Clause') said
among other things:

> We are met here today to commemorate our national Heroes'
> Day. We are, today, going down the corridor of time and
> renewing our acquaintance with the heroes of Afrika's past—
> those men and women who nourished the tree of African
> freedom and independence with their blood; those great Sons
> and Daughters of Afrika who died in order that we may be free
> in the land of our birth. We are here today to dedicate our
> lives to the cause of Afrika, to establish contact, beyond the
> grave, with the great African heroes and to assure them that
> their struggle was not in vain. We are here, Sons and
> Daughters of our beloved land, to drink from the fountain of
> African achievement, to remember the men and women who
> begot us, to remind ourselves of where we come from and
> restate our goals.
>
> We are here to draw inspiration from the Heroes of Thaba
> Bosiu, Isandlwana, Sandile's Kop, Keiskama Hoek, Blood
> River and numerous other battlefields where our forefathers fell
> before the bullets of the foreign invader. We are here to draw
> inspiration from the Sons and Daughters of Afrika who gave
> their all to the cause and were physically broken in the strug-
> gle. We are met here, Sons and Daughters of Afrika to take
> trowel in our right hand and a shield and sword in our left. We
> are gathered here, today to reiterate our resolve to declare total
> war against the demigods of white supremacy. We are here, to
> serve an ultimatum on the forces of oppression...[7]

What Africans know about South Africa is thus in sharp contradiction to what Europeans have said and written. But let us momentarily leave this controversy and try to trace the history of the Black people of Azania. First, it is important to note that there is a theory that the ancestors of the present Black people of Azania came from Egypt. It also seems that while there they lived for some time with the Hebrew people (Jews). This theory is strengthened by the fact that Africans have many customs common to the Old Testament Jewish 'culture' such as a circumcision, atonement for crime or sin by blood, raising a family for a dead brother and so on.

D.E. Ellenberger and J.C. Macgregor agree with this theory. They point out that the Basuto women of olden days, under their traditional dress, wore a girdle of twisted grass called thethana round their loins. They think that this word is derived from the Hebrew word thana meaning a fig tree,[8] which according to Gensis 3:7 was the tree whose leaves Adam and Eve wore to cover their nakedness.

The belief that Africans came from the North and were influenced by Hebrews seems to be also confirmed by a Venda tradition. The old Venda people of Azania had a sounding drum. It was equivalent to the Hebrew ark of the Lord. The Venda Africans called their 'ark' *Ngoma-Lungundulu* in their language. They kept and used their sounding drum or ark almost in the same way that the Hebrews kept the ark of the Lord.

In their book *The History of the Basuto—Ancient and Modern*, D.E. Ellenberger and J.C. Macgregor say that except for the Bushmen it was the Bantu (the present black people of South Africa) who first occupied this country. Although it is always difficult to give actual dates as the history of the Black people of South Africa is mainly based on tradition, the two writers have identified the first inhabitants of South Africa as the Iron Age people. The Barolong danced in honour of a hammer and iron. Ellenberger and Macgregor quote Rev Lemue as saying that Morolong actually means a blacksmith. The Barolong, the Bafokeng and other Bantu tribes are believed to have arrived from the North over two thousand years ago (compared with Jan Van Riebeeck who arrived in South Africa in 1652 around three hundred and thirty years ago).[9] In South Africa the Iron Age Black Africans were more numerous than the San people who are believed to have arrived from the North over three thousand years ago.

It does not seem that the Black people of Azania entered their present country by invasion or bloodshed. The San people (Bushmen) never resisted them. Instead they fraternized with them and intermarriages between them and the Black people of Azania was common. In fact, as late as 1833 King Moshoeshoe married two San women as junior wives.

There were also many marriages between the Bantu (Sotho group) and the San people who were living with them along the Vaal areas in the present Orange Free State about 1450 A.D. However one such marriage, caused trouble. A chief of the Bafokeng tribe married a San woman as his principal wife. This was bitterly opposed by the chief's people. They said that according to custom he was to marry a Mofokeng woman as his senior wife. People who think their blood is 'royal' have always been fussy all over the world. For instance, in the 20th century marriages such as those of Sir Seretse Khama of Botswana and Princess Margaret sister of Queen Elizabeth II have been opposed.

The Mofokeng chief was obstinate, and despite the opposition he married the San women. While he lived things proceeded unperturbed. But when he died the tribe refused to be ruled by his sons born of the San woman. The situation deteriorated to such an extent that the sons of the San woman left with such of their father's people as were loyal to them. They crossed into Natal and finally settled with a Xhosa tribe called the Tembus in what is today's Cape Province. They were absorbed into the Xhosa society and completely lost their identity.[10] Chief Tyali of the Xhosa is believed to have been a descendant of the San woman who married the Mofokeng chief. It is interesting to note that the Vundla clan in the Cape Province, though they are Xhosas, consider themselves related to the Bafokeng of Mmutla. They have adopted the hare as their totem and do not eat its meat.

According to Ellenberger and Macgregor other sons of the Mofokeng chief obviously by black African women also left the Vaal after the tribe's disintegration. They moved to what is today the district of Heidleburg which was then called Tebang by the indigenous Africans. Ellenberger and Macgregor also mention other off-spring of chief Tabane and Mathulare. These were the Bapedi, the Makholokoe, the Baphuthing, the Basia and the Batlokoa who lived in areas including where the town of Pretoria stands today.

Lesotho lost much of its territory to the Boers after the 1836 Great Trek but before Moshoeshoe came to weld the *Basotho* into a modern nation during the 'Wars of Shaka', huge tracts of land in present Lesotho and parts of the Orange Free State were occupied by the Lesotho people. This excludes the Barolong and other Bantu tribes who lived in the Orange Free State before the arrival of Jan van Riebeeck in 1652.

The *Basotho* people of Lesotho had leaders like Monaheng,

Mokheseng and Mohlomi. Mokheseng died in 1860. Monaheng, his father, was also called Kali, which was not his real name. He was given the name of Monaheng by the San people with whom he lived. This is another sign of peaceful coexistence between the Iron Age Black people of Azania and their San brothers.

Another interesting figure that emerges from the history of the Basotho is Mohlomi. He was both a great philosopher and administrator. But unlike the philosopher and administrator, King Ngconde of the Xhosa Africans, Mohlomi was also a roving diplomat, preaching peace and brotherhood among the African people he met in Southern Africa.

Mohlomi lived in a place called Ngodiloe by the Basotho people. It is now Ficksburg and no longer part of Lesotho but part of the Orange Free State. This was the result of the wars launched by the Boer trekkers after 1836. Mohlomi's importance in history lies in the fact that it was he who taught Moshoeshoe the philosophy of peace and made him a great diplomat and statesman. To this day the Basotho people have a national slogan, *Khotso ke Nala* (peace brings prosperity).

Genealogy of the Bapedi

Approximate Year

1540	Tabane Matlaisane (chief of Bamutsha)
1570	Lilale also called Mopeli
1600	Molise Le-Lellateng Mampuru (Chief of Mafefe)
1630	chief of Bamakau Moroa-Motsha
1660	Kotope Thulare
1690	'Malekutu Sekuati
1720	Sekhukhuni 1
1750	Moroa-Motsha II also called Kholoko
1780	Sekhukuni II

Genealogy of the Bafokeng

Approximate Date
980

A.D.	Napo
1010	Setsete
1040	'Mutle
1070	Phogole
1100	Mare
1130	Khulo
1160	Molubiane

1190	Phate
1220	Maphate
1250	Mafole
1280	Mekhesi
1310	Morapeli
1340	Mpuru
1370	Tsoane
1400	Ramoroa
1430	Sekete I
1460	Fokeng (or Phokeng)
1490	Ramoroa II
1520	Sekete II
1550	Mogono
1580	Magobe
1610	Monoe
1640	Sekete III
1670	Liale I
1700	Ramoroa III
1730	'Mutle Sekete IV Katane
1760	Liale II Nameng Noge
1790	Tumahole
1820	Molahlegi, viz.

In 1905 Mokhatle was chief of the Bafokeng.[11]

It must be noted that this genealogy or family tree is based on the assumption that African chiefs lived for only thirty years. But the truth of the matter is that African leaders lived longer. Many lived for as long as seventy years, while King Khama of the Bamagwato lived even longer. Napo therefore lived longer than thirty years with his people in present day Azania from around eight hundred twenty A.D.

References:
1. A.H. Keane, *The Boer States*, p. 147.
2. J.A. Williamson, *The British Empire and Commonwealth*, p. 276.
3. *Ibid*.
.4 Dube David, as quoted in *The Rise of Azania*, P.11.
5. James Evans, *'Apartheid As Idolatry'*, in *Christianity and Crisis*, 14 December 1981.
6. *Azania News*, June 1967.
7. Mangaliso R. Sobukwe, State of the Nation Address, 30 July 1959.

8. D.E. Ellenberger and J.C. Macgregor, *History of the Basuto—Ancient and Modern*, p. 15.
9. *Ibid*., p. 18.
10. *Ibid*., p.19.
11. *Ibid*., p. 349.
12. *Ibid*., p. 357

2. Portuguese Met Azanians in 1497

In 1487 Captain Bartholomew Diaz reached the Cape coast situated at the southern tip of Africa. A heavy storm harassed the Portuguese so menacingly that he called the area the Cape of Storms. However a more optimistic King Emmanuel, changed the name to the 'Cape of Good Hope'. Although it is unclear whether Diaz met the indigenous people of Azania, it is unlikely for he spent all his time at sea. His successor, Vasco da Gama, who landed in Azania on Christmas Day 1497 and called it Natal (Land of Nativity in commemoration of Christ's birthday), definitely met the African people. However whether they were Khoi or Iron Age Black indigenous Africans is unclear. Many Europeans have found it difficult to distinguish Africans from Khoi. Jan van Riebeeck himself met the Khoisan people in 1652, but they did not know the difference between the Khoi and San people until 1685!

According to G.Mackeurtan, author of *The Cradle of Natal* (1497-1845), and at one time the King of England's representative in South Africa, Vasco da Gama landed at a bay north of the Cape. He says that the Hottentots (Khoi) had at first provided da Gama with beef which he described 'as sweet as that of Portugal,' and entertained his crew with pastoral flutes making 'pretty harmony for Negroes' who are not expected to be musicians.'[1]

In explaining this apparent confusion about Natal and the bay north of the Cape, Mackeurtan points out that modern Natal until Zululand was added to it in 1897 has always meant the land between the Umtamvuna River on the south and the Tugela on the north.[2] Of course, it is a misnomer to speak of modern Natal and Zululand because almost the whole of today's Natal was the country of the black people called Zulus.

King Shaka himself a much later ruler of the Zulus had his seat of government only 125 miles from the Port of Natal. His people knew the port as Thekwini. The name changed to Durban in honour of a

British military leader Sir Benjamin D'Urban during the wars of resistance by the indigenous people. Mackeurtan added 'This name Natal really belongs not to the people of Natal but to natives of Pondoland.'[3]

This is contradicted by Peter Becker in his book *Rule of Fear*. When he wrote:

> In the early decades of the nineteenth century during the tyran-nical rule of Shaka King of the Zulu, the South African territory today known as Zululand and Natal were studded with great military kraals garrisoned by powerful, war-lusty regiments.[4]

For the purpose of this discussion it is not necessary to wrangle about whether or not Natal was in Natal or in Pondoland in the Cape Province. The important thing is that the Portuguese landed on the Blackman's land in 1497. It must also be mentioned that the first Africans that Vasco da Gama met in 1497 seem to have not been Khoi (Hottentots) as Mackeurtan describes them. These people were the descendants of the Iron Age Black people of Azania. Byrant writer of *Older Times in Zululand and Natal* confirms this when he says that on December 1497 A.D. a Bantu man emerging from the dense bush on the sea-shores near Durban, beheld the wonderful sight of Vasco da Gama the first known white man to be seen by Africans in South Africa.

Portuguese Voyages Round South Africa

Many of their ships were wrecked. From the survivors of these ships much can be learned about the earlier occupation of Azania by the Iron Age Black people.

For instance, in 1552 one of the largest ships, *Saint John*, was wreck-ed by a fierce storm as it neared Cape at Umtamvuna. Much merchan-dise was lost. But after salvaging what they could, the Portuguese sur-vivors gathered on the beach surrounded by the goods they managed to save. Some of them began to nurse their wounded and perhaps their dying. Three days after this, it is recorded that nine Africans appeared on a hill and watched the Portuguese survivors below the hill on the shore, 'but they withdrew as if afraid.'[5]

Some five days later these Africans reappeared again. This time they were many and driving a cow. They went close to the ship's survivors and showed by signs that they wanted to exchange their cow for iron. 'When the Portuguese offered a few nails, the Africans went wild with delight; even at that early time the meaning and possibilities of a ship were known to these Africans, but by what means than by tradition of trade north with Arab dhows is unknown.'[6]

Two years after the wreck of Saint John another ship called Saint Benedict was wrecked in the area of Mbashe River in 1554. It had 473 passengers and was laden with a large store of precious goods. On the 27 April the same year the survivors of this ship walked a long distance and reached the site of Saint John ship which had been wrecked in 1552. They found many remains of that ship-wreck. They were amazed to find a number of local African homes furnished with crockery and other goods salvaged from the wrecked Portuguese ship.[7]

This was not to be their last experience. On the 27 May they reached the lagoon in Durban which according to T.V. Bulpin, 'the Africans knew as *eThekwini*, but the Portuguese called Pescaria meaning the Fisheries.'[8]

It was called by this name because of a number of fish places which were operated by the African fishermen. Here the Portuguese survivors to their surprise met two former slaves of Saint John ship. Through these men they were able to influence the local Africans to trade for fish and food. But when they asked the former slaves to join them this was rejected. The ex-slaves were too happy in their newly found freedom to desire the yoke of slavery.

After the Portuguese had failed to persuade the former slaves to join them, they left. As they were leaving they met a group of Africans emerging from the bush, among them was a 'naked man with assegais upon his back and was in no way different from the rest of them, until by his hair and speech we found him to be a Portuguese named Rodridge Tristao.' He was the survivor of *Saint John*, ship wrecked in 1552.[9]

Another Portuguese ship, the *Saint Alberto*, was wrecked south of Umtata River in March 1593. Its survivors reported that the inhabitants of the land South of this river were Xhosas. These Africans were dressed in mantle of ox hide and wore sandals. They cultivated millet (amabele or amazimba) and possessed large herds of cattle. They lived in villages of low round huts. These survivors also noted that the Iron Age Black Africans north of another river the Tugela were skilled workers in iron.[10]

In 1687 a vessel, the *Noord*, was sent by the Dutch East India Company in the Cape to search for European survivors of wrecked ships. In January 1689 the crews of this vessel found two survivors of the *Stavenisse*. They had wandered back to the site of the wreckage. Another man was found living with Pondos of the Cape Province. He was an old Portuguese sailor a survivor of a ship wrecked along the Pondo coast about 1649, now married to an African woman and a father. The European crews of the *Noord* tried to 'rescue' him by persuading him to go and live with the settlers who had already built the provision station at Capetown. But he refused to be 'rescued.' He only spoke the African language: 'having forgotten everything else, his God included,' lamented one writer.[11]

Africans Friendly to Portuguese Sailors

Another striking feature of the Portuguese contact with the Africans of 'South Africa' is that the indigenous people always received them with great hospitality: a stark contrast to the way they received the Boer settlers. In 1689 the crews of the *Noord* from today's Maputo met the natives at the Port (Durban). Although these Africans were without the fear of God, one writer notes, that they were friendly and provided food and fresh water. The vessel obtained bread, milk, beans, fowls and pumpkin. Some of the *Noord's* crew walked a few miles along the sea coast to the Umngeni River, which was running low. There were indigenous Africans along its banks and they supplied the travellers with food and at sunset led them across the country back to the *Noord*; 'singing as they went.'[12] This was typical African hospitality. No wonder the Portuguese sailors never forgot to mention it to their comrades.

The Europeans were often amazed by the treatment the Africans gave them. For instance, after the *Johanna* was shipwrecked in 1683, eighty survivors were stranded. They sought help and shelter and met natives. 'Though they were reputed great Barbarians... they treated these stranded people with such civility and humanity than some nations that I know who pretend much religion and politeness,' one of the Portuguese survivors said.[13] These Africans were not only liberal but they are reported to have helped the strangers and asked for very moderate rewards in return, never taking the slightest advantage of the stranded strangers in need.

On the 23 January 1689 the *Noord* left Port Natal (Durban). On its way south a survivor of the *Staveniesse* was picked up. These rescued men reported that in all their wanderings they had seen only one white man. He was a Portuguese survivor of the *Nosa Sanhora de Atalaya* shipwreck in 1647. Remnants of the ship were still to be seen on the shore in 1689. The Portuguese sailors had seen a Portuguese survivor living among the Pondo tribesmen. He had been 'circumcised, and had a wife and children, cattle and land... '[14]

The sailors of a ship *Happy Deliverance* landed on the coast of modern Natal about 1756 (eighty years before the Boer Great Trek). These sailors found the 'natives an honest, open harmless and friendly people.' They observed that these Africans divided what they had, no matter how little. The sailors described these inhabitants as being very like Hottentots except they were more 'innocent, benevolent and sincere.' They were also without jealousy for they 'left their sisters and daughters whole days with the strangers while rambling about woods... ' The English sailors were extremely surprised to find among these 'savages who were quite black with wooly hair' a youth about twelve or fourteen perfectly white, with regular European features. He was treated as a servant, sent on errands. The boy was no albino or white kaffir.[15]

Mackeurtan points out that the survivors of wrecked ships often suffered great hardships. He says that some of the rescued survivors passed southwards from what he calls Abambo of Natal through various tribes of Hottentots. Besides the Hottentots he mentions the Temboos (*AbaTembu*), Mapondomise (*AmaPondomse*), Mapondo (*AmaPondo*), Magosse (*AmaXhosa*). He also mentions the Maligryhas whom he describes as a Hottentot tribe. He says that they were very unfriendly to Europeans although he does not give the reasons for their hostility. If it is true that these Khoi people were hostile to the white people, it must have been after their long contact with the settlers of Dutch origin in the Cape Province. This particular group of Europeans was terribly unscrupulous with these Khoi Africans.

The Portuguese and other European survivors of wrecked ships not only show the friendship with which they were received by the Africans, but also the way they lived. For instance, Mackeurtan speaks of a Xhosa chief Magama (probably Maqoma) 'a friendly, good-hearted young fellow... ' He says that when this chief died his people put away all their ornaments and kept away from their women for a year. Of course, this is how most Africans mourned their great dead.

Anthropologists and any other people who know the habits and customs of Africans will agree that these people who were met by the Portuguese survivors and others on wrecked ships could not have been but what are today called Bantu. The theory therefore, prevalent especially among apartheid politicians and others that Azania was 'empty' when the settlers 'occupied' it, is untenable.

References:
1. G. Mackeurtan, *The Cradle Days of Natal (1497-1845)*, p. 7.
2. *Ibid.*, p. 14.
3. *Ibid.*
4. Peter Becker, *Rule of Fear*, p. 3.
5. T.V. Bulpin, *To the Shores of Natal*, p. 29.
6. *Ibid.*, p. 29-30.
7. *Ibid.*, p. 31.
8. *Ibid.*, p. 32.
9. *Ibid.*
10. *Azania News*, 18 May/1 June 1967.
11. G. Mackeurtan, *The Cradle Days of Natal (1497-1845)*, p. 64.
12. *Ibid.*, p. 63.
13. *Ibid.*, p. 54-55.
14. *Ibid.*, p. 64.
15. *Ibid.*, p. 82.

3. The Khoisan Influence of Bantu Culture

Centuries before the descendants of Jan van Riebeeck landed on the southern tip of the blackman's continent there had been social interaction between the Iron Age Black people of Azania and the Khoisan people (Hottentots and Bushmen). At least one Portuguese survivor found living with the Pondo Africans was 'circumcised.' Traditionally, circumcision among the Black people of Azania was the highest institution of learning. It was a school where boys were being prepared to become real men. Anyone who was not circumcised was regarded as a 'boy' (*inkwenkwe, leqai*). The uncircumcised were despised and could not be given any responsibility in society. Sometimes circumcision was enforced.

The custom of circumcision was practised by almost all the Azanias—Venda, Bapedi, Basotho, Batswana, Xhosa and many others. Among the Zulus, circumcision was done away with by Shaka, but his own father Senzangakhona had been circumcised.

The importance of circumcision in this discussion is that there is a strong theory that this custom was copied by the Iron Age Black people from the San people (Bushmen). Ellenberger and Macgregor through information recieved from the Basotho in Lesotho were told that the custom of circumcision was copied from the San people.[1]

Of course, some people will argue that the custom of circumcision was introduced by the Egyptians probably through the Jewish people with whom they lived. The Jews had been given this command in the Bible. Then it is possible that when some Africans left Egypt many years ago they brought this custom with them. But the theory that it was introduced by the San is logical, particularly in view of the fact that African communities which did not have contact with the San people directly or indirectly did not practise circumcision.

But even if the theory that Africans in Azania borrowed the custom of circumcision from the San people was unacceptable to some people, it would not invalidate the fact that the Iron Age Black Africans did live side by side with the San people for thousands of years. In present day South Africa there are many 'light' skinned Africans. Their complexion is different from that of the so-called 'Cape Coloureds' who are the offspring of European settlers by miscegenation. The 'light' complexion of some Black people of Azania clearly confirms that for many years there was intermarriage between some 'Bantu' Africans and Khoisan people. This 'light' colour is particularly conspicuous among many Xhosa and Sotho speaking Africans.

In the Cape Province for instance, there was much intermarriage between the Xhosa and the Khoi people while there was more intermarriage between the Sothos (Barolong, Basotho, Bapedi, Batswana and others) and Khoisan. Intermarriage between the Xhosa Africans and the Khoi Africans, in some cases it was so common that *Amagqunukwebe* (a Xhosa tribe) has been described by some writers as half-Xhosa and half-Hottentots.[2]

To this day among the Xhosa such clan names as Amagqwashu, Amacira and AmaSukwini can still be found among the Amagqunukwebe tribe. They have become completely Xhosa. But they greet each other by referring to the Khoi people. *'Ncocho, Lawu'* (honouranle one of the Khoi). They speak of their women as *Amalawukazi ampundu zibomvu'* (the she Khoi people who have fair red buttocks). Some of the Khoi people lived in today's Middle Drift in the Cape Province. This was round what has been corrupted as *Amatola* Mountains. *Amatola* actually means people who have an advanced knowledge of African medicines. It is where a number of Khoi traditional doctors lived. And *Amahlathi kaHoho* (a place near Kingwillamston meaning the forests of Hoho) is also of interest. The forests were named after a Khoi queen whose name was *Hoho* — centuries before 1652.

Templeton M. Ntantala for many years a prominent rugby player in the Cape Western Region and later a deputy chairman of the Revolutionary Command of the Pan Africanist Congress (POQO) comes from the Amangqunukwebe tribe. The Xhosa people were also known as 'Chobona' as Peter Dreyer writes, 'These Chobona were in fact the Xhosa, who intermingled with the Khoi in the Eastern Cape, and the suggestions of their paramountcy raises some interesting questions.'[3]

It is not surprising that the Dutch settlers first met large numbers of the Xhosa Africans east of the Gamtoos River, near the present city of Bayi renamed Port Elizabeth by the settlers. There has always been an attempt to separate the Khoi from Africans just as there is an attempt to separate 'Coloureds' from Africans although 'Coloureds' are in digenous Azanians.

The Khoisans and Bantu Languages

The languages of both the 'Bantu' and the Khoisan people show that they lived together many years prior to the European arrival in Azania. The Khoisan languages greatly influenced the languages of Xhosa and Southern Sotho speakers. Today one of the chief characteristics of these languages such as Pedi and Tswana; is the click sounds. Miriam Makeba that Nightingale of Azania is well known for her click song *Uqongqothwane*.

Clicks found in the African languages such as Xhosa, Zulu and Southern Sotho clearly confirm that the Africans of the Cape Province, Natal and the Orange Free State lived side by side with their Khoisan neighbours many years ago. For instance, in Xhosa and Zulu languages the following Khoisan clicks are found:

/ = c is a dental click
! = q the palatal click
// = x which is the lateral click

These click sounds may be voiced, unvoiced or aspirated in their articulation as in the following examples:

!keib (cloth) Xhosa iqhiya (really means headscarve)
/nom (smile) Xhosa ncuma
/kam (urinate) Xhosa and Zulu chama
/e (ask for) Xhosa and Zulu cela

Other interesting examples of the influence of the Khoisan languages on the vocabulary of Xhosa and Zulu are:

/heba-b (grave) = Xhosa and Zulu ingcwaba
/a-b (grass) = Xhosa ingca
// are (left) = Xhosa and Zulu inxele
lari-b (river) = Xhosa iGqili (Orange River)

The language of the Basotho Africans was greatly influenced by the Khoisan people particularly, by the San with whom they lived together in the present Orange Free State and vicinity, and intermarried. The click sound ! = q is found in Southern Sotho words such as *qala* (begin or tease) *qeta* (finish) *qamaka* (look around) *qibi* (an instrument of San origin) *qhala* (scatter or spill) and in names such as *Senqu* (Orange River) *Qualing, Quthing* etc.

However, it should be noted that Xhosa has more click sounds than

Zulu, a curious phenomenon. Some writers like Ellenberger and Macgregor have suggested that there was lack of contact between the Zulu Africans and the San. Then where did the Zulus get their clicks? Was it indirectly through the Xhosas? But it seems that like all other Africans, the Zulus got their clicks sounds from the San and Khoi people with whom they lived, for many centuries before the arrival of Jan van Riebeeck. Two reasons suggest this: firstly, there is a widespread story about the San people which has been passed by one generation to another generation. It is said that when a San met a black African, he would ask: 'At what distance did you see me? (*Umpone ke sa tla le kae?*) If the answer was 'I saw you when you were still many many miles away,' the San would be very happy; but if it was 'I saw you when already very near!', the San would look sad. The old people gave the explanation that the San people were very short but did not like to be told that they were short. They took this to mean that they were inferior—hence the joy when they were told they were seen a long distance away as this implied that they were not so short after all! The old Zulu people say the San often asked: *Ungibonabon'ephi?*

The second reason arises from T.V. Bulpin confirmation that there existed an ivory trade involving English traders like Fyn. 'This tribe had learnt elephant hunting from the Bushmen, including the secrets of the use of the bow and poisoned arrows, and they scoured Natal in search of tusks. In Bushmen fashion, when they killed an elephant the whole tribe would camp around the corpse until they had totally consumed it.'[4]

Religious Influence of Khoi People

The Khoi people not only influenced the Xhosa language, but their religious life as well. For instance, the Xhosa word for God is *Thixo*. As can be clearly seen this word comes from the Khoi language. Another Xhosa word for God is *Qamata*. The click sound confirms the great influence the Khoisan people had on the religious life of the Xhosa Africans. It is unusual that people who do not know each other and are perhaps hostile to each other can influence each other in religious matters except at the point of the gun and economic stranglehold.

If the Xhosa had not lived with Khoi people for many years, how did they come to accept the elements of the Khoi religion into their own life? How did they come to call their God by names borrowed from the Khoi people—*Thixo* and *Qamata*? It must be remembered that the Xhosa Africans were far numerous than the Khoi people. How did then this

Khoi minority influence the vast Xhosa majority? It must also be noted that to the Africans of those days religion was a matter of life and death. It was something that was not lightly adopted or changed for fear that ancestors or *Umdali* (Creator) might be angered and send a calamity as punishment.

The only reasonable explanation why the Khoi influenced the Xhosas in religious matters is that there was just great harmony between the Xhosa Africans and the Khoi Africans. Of course, it would be naive to suggest that there were no quarrels among the Xhosa and Khoi Africans. Quarrels are everywhere. But relations between the two groups were far friendlier than the apartheid historians are prepared to admit.

Christianity came to South Africa over two hundred years ago, but it is known that to this day the Dutch Reformed Church in South Africa is the most hated church. Many times African leaders have asked members of their parties to quit the Dutch Reformed Church. At Church Conferences reports are often heard complaining that apartheid is hindering the Gospel. To influence people religiously one has to have their confidence and live in harmony with them. This is how the Khoi came to influence so many aspects of the Xhosa life. In fact, even for language, English has been more influential among the Africans in South Africa than the language of the Boers—Afrikaans. This shows that the relations between the indigenous Africans and the descendants of Jan van Riebeeck are not as good as they were between the Xhosa and Khoi Africans.

Archaeology Refutes Apartheid Historians

Archaeologists like D.W. Phillipson have confirmed that about 100 A.D. hunting people who used the stone tools and were of what is called bushboskop physical type, were wide-spread in Southern Africa. During the first 1000 years A.D. there is evidence of iron, gold, and copper mining and smelting: pottery, cattle and sheep rearing and crop growing in many parts of Zambia, Rhodesia and Transvaal in Azania. In Swaziland iron mining and smelting was started as early as 500 A.D.[5] Other sources record an earlier date.

Many archaeologists have shown that the Iron Age Black people of the Transvaal were established at Palaborwa in the 9th century and at Mapungubwe the centre of the earlier great civilization of the Black people of Azania in about 1400 A.D.

Now, the argument has been raised about these Iron Age people. Were they Khoi or San (Hottentots or Bushmen)? Facts reveal that the people were latter-day descendants of the Stone Age people of Azania. The Khoi on the other hand were cattle and sheep-keepers. They were also pottery-makers, but they never practised agriculture or became iron workers. The Iron Age people of Azania, therefore, were not Khoi or San Africans but ancestors of the present Black people of Azania so called Bantu.

D.W. Phllipson has confirmed this theory. He holds that the elements of the Iron Age culture were imported into South Africa by Black people during the first 1000 years A.D. He suggests that during this time the Iron Age culture spread as far as the Transvaal and Natal and a little farther.[6] Monica Wilson an outstanding anthropologist seems to agree with D.W. Phillipson's findings about the Iron Age people being ancestors of the present Black people of Azania. But she points out that, like the San people of Azania, they descended from the Stone Age societies. But unlike the San they acquired pastoral farming.[7]

Archaeologists like R.J. Mason author of *Prehistory of the Transvaal* and D.W. Phillipson have said that farther south in the Transvaal, Iron Age occupation distinct from the Early Iron Age tradition seems to have been worked on the Witwatersrand by about 1025 A.D.[8]

Another interesting archaeological discovery about the Iron Age Black people of Azania is that made by Beaumount. As D.W. Phillipson puts it, at the Castle Peak in western Swaziland, Beaumont has obtained a single date of the 4th and 5th century A.D (Y−1712) from charcoal associated with sherds of vessels. Phillipson has also mentioned a series of dates obtained by van der Merwe from iron and copper working sites at Palaborwa in the eastern Transvaal. He says that the mine workings were found at Loolekop. They were 70 feet and dates in the 7th to the 11th centuries A.D.[9]

The Iron Age Africans occupied the Transvaal and the Orange Free State many years before Jan van Riebeeck made any appearance in Azania on the 6 April 1652. Brian Fagan Professor of Anthropology at the University of California in his article, *The Later Iron Age in South Africa* quotes several sources showing that travellers like A. Moffat and J. Campbell saw the 'stone towns' of Iron Age Bantu Black Africans in the provinces of today's South Africa. Brian Fagan's article corroborates the African tradition which has been passed from generation to generation. That is that the Black people of Azania occupied and lived in this beautiful and rich country many years before Jan van Riebeeck was born or ever dreamed of being an employee of the Dutch East India Company.

Professor Fagan says,

For many years it was assumed by the ignorant that the Bantu speaking peoples crossed the Limpopo at approximately the same time as Van Riebeeck landed at the Cape. This view, sometimes still glimpsed in obscure or nationalistic literature has been completely disproved by the research of Revil Mason and Monica Wilson and others.[10]

Fagan goes on to say that Revil Mason has examined many Iron Age sites in the Transvaal. He made extensive use of aerial photographs to locate stone structures. He found a number of radio carbon dates for various settlements. According to Fagan, Revil Mason's excavations on the Witwatersrand revealed that Iron Age people have been in the Transvaal for over 1000 years.[11] Mason published his work in *The Origin of the South African Societies* in 1965. This therefore, means that the Africans were in the Transvaal earlier than 965 A.D. Incidentally, Monica Wilson has also established the much earlier occupation of the Cape Province by the Xhosa Africans.

According to Xhosa-speaking African writers like J.H.Soga, King Xhosa ruled in the Cape Province about 1553 while S.E. Mqhayi author of *Ityala laMawele* suggests an earlier date. Despite the difference in the dates by these writers and others, facts demonstrate the antiquity of the settlement of the Xhosas in the present Cape Province.

References:
1. G. Mackeurtan, *The Cradle Days of Natal (1497-1845)*, p. 65.
2. Eric A. Walker, *A History of Southern Africa*, p. 98.
3. Peter Dreyer, *MARTYRS AND FANATICS South Africa and Human Destiny*, p. 81.
4. T.V. Bulpin, *To the Shores of Natal*, p. 68.
5. Leonard Thompson (ed.), *African Societies in Southern Africa*, p. 6.
6. *Ibid.*, p. 8.
7. *Ibid.*, p. 9.
8. *Ibid.*, p. 36.
9. *Ibid.*, p. 36.
10. *Ibid.*, p. 50.
11. *Ibid.*, p. 51.

4. Jan Van Riebeeck and the Khoisan People

In 1503 Antonia de Saldnha sailed into today's Table Bay in Capetown. He is said to have climbed Table Mountain and met the Khoi Africans. In 1509 Don Francisco de Almeida, a retired Portuguese officer sailed from the Malbar coast in Asia to Africa with a small squadron, making a stopover in Mozambique. From there he proceeded to today's Cape Province arriving in February 1510. The Khoi Africans met him on the beach and bought some pieces of calico and iron from him.

A misunderstanding between these Africans and Portuguese sailors developed. The Portuguese sailors of those early days considered themselves invincible, and were arrogant in their dealings with the Khoi Africans. The Africans reacted. As one writer put it, 'The Khoi were not to be bullied with impunity, and blows were struck. De Almeida, said to have been humane man by comparison with some of his contemporaries, was persuaded against his will that it was necessary to teach these savages a lesson. Accordingly, before dawn on the morning of March 1st 1510, he landed with a hundred and fifty men to administer it (African land).'[1]

This led to the first war between Africans and Europeans on the Azanian soil. The Portuguese invaders armed with swords, lances and cross bows marched on the Khoi villages and took possession of their cattle. They siezed the children they found as hostages. A fierce battle ensured. A number of Khoi warriors armed with assegais charged the Portuguese, the Azanians won the first war with the Whites. The enemy retreated and sixty- five Portuguese lay dead, among them Don Francisco de Almeida.

This was one of the most glorious victories by Africans in the battle field against the white invaders in Azania. This victory stopped the European invaders and aggressors from venturing into Azania for at least 150 years. It was only in 1667 after the arrival of Jan van Riebeeck that the second war between Africans and Europeans was fought.

The English also sailed to Azania before the arrival of Jan van Riebeeck. In 1580 it was Francis Drake and his crew. In 1591 three ships sailed out of Plymouth under the command of Admiral George Raymond for Azania. Several others followed later. They desperately needed trade with the Khoi. Consequently the first African to learn English was a Khoi called Xhora. Other historians call him Quore. He returned from an English course in England in 1614. Xhore could now speak fluent English and help the white traders who bought Khoi cattle and sheep for almost nothing. On arrival back in Azania, he left the Whites and went to live with his people. Once he was there, the prices of the Khoi cattle went up. This disturbed the exploiting European traders who were not paying fair prices for the African cattle.

One of them remarked that it had been better if Xhore had never seen England. There he had discovered that brass which was used to purchase cattle from the Khoi Africans was a base and cheap commodity in England. In fact, the Khoi people now wanted to barter their cattle for copper and not for brass as before.

Who Was Jan Van Riebeeck?

The Dutch East India Company was founded in 1602. By 1604 it had already established bases in Bantam, Java and the coveted Malaccas which were all rich in spices. The Company also seized Amboyna and half of Timor in Asia and unsuccessfully tried to gain a foothold in present day Mozambique in Africa.

Eric A. Walker suggests that it was not the object of the Dutch East India Company to colonize. The main purpose of the Company was to monopolise trade. Competition was simply not permitted. 'The massacre of Amboyna, the seizure of Malacca, the exclusion of the English from the spice Islands by the Treaty of Breda, the closing of Java to the English and French were all stages in the stranglehold which the Dutch Company acquired upon the spice-trade of the East Indies... the Company guarded the spices most rigorously and strove to destroy all rival traders whether native or European, Coen himself wiped out the people of Banda... '[2]

Walker continues to say that though there was no native industry to be destroyed at the Cape and no spice-trade to guard, the spirit and methods of the Dutch East India administration were applied in the Cape in full force. The directors of the Dutch East India Company meant to keep the trade monopoly.[3]

In short the officials of the Dutch East India Company like Jan van Riebeeck were not philanthropists out to uplift the indigenous people of Azania. They were like all capitalists and traders out to make money by whatever means necessary. Jan van Riebeeck came to South Africa in 1652 to establish a 'provision station' for the sole purpose of making money for this Company. Monopoly goes hand in hand with colonialism. In 1647 a ship, the *Haarlem* wrecked in Table Mountain. The Dutch survivors managed to get to a shore and grow some vegetables. Later when they arrived in Holland, Nicholaas Proot and Leender Janssen reported favourably about the need and possibility of establishing a 'provision station' that could supply fresh food to sailors round the Cape coast. Janssen and Proot had been with Jan van Riebeeck on the *Haarlem*.

Jan van Riebeeck was therefore selected as the man to carry out the important work of founding the station where Capetown now stands. The Company gave Jan van Riebeeck instructions: he was to build a *fort* to bear the name of 'Good Hope'. He was to plant a garden in the 'best and fattest land'. If necessary he would use the same crude methods that the Company through Coen had used in Asia. He was instructed to live on good terms with the indigenous Africans 'for the sake of trade.'[4]

What kind of man was Jan van Riebeeck? He has been described by Eric A. Walker as 'thick-set, determined little man of thirty-three, tanned by the sun of West Indies, Siam and China and hard-bitten with the winds of Greenland.'[5] His attitude toward the indigenous people seems to have been very unfriendly. The first report he gave about them in Holland was very uncomplimentary for a man who was about to have at least business dealings with them. He described these people as a 'faithless rabble.' It is difficult to know how Jan van Riebeeck came to this prejudiced conclusion because it was not until 1685 that the settlers began to distinguish the Khoi from the San people. And it was 13 years after Jan van Riebeeck himself had left the 'provision station.'

This seems to prove that, Jan van Riebeeck though claiming much religion and civilization and highly regarded by his present apartheid descendants as a man worth monuments to honour him, he was in fact a man of preconceived ideas and much prejudice. It is also significant that Jan van Riebeeck and his colleagues regarded the Khoisan people as simply 'dull, stupid, lazy and stinking.'[6] Yet these men had been living for thousands of years and able to look after themselves and had never begged food from the settlers. Instead as we shall see later it was these settlers who were always begging or even cheating the Khoi Africans to sell their cattle to them.

Commenting on the dealings of the settlers with the San people, Walker says:

> The Bushmen were relics of the Stone Age. Their neighbours
> (Jan van Riebeeck and the like) may be pardoned for doubting
> whether they were quite human, for they were little sallow
> folk, barely four feet high, their heads adorned with peppercorn
> tufts of hair and lobeless ears... their triangular fox-like faces
> almost innocent of beards. Their twinkling eyes were deep-set
> beneath upright foreheads, their noses broad and low-rooted,
> ...and their slender limbs and tiny feet ill-fitted to the bear pro-
> tuberant stomachs of the men or the pendulous breasts and fat
> buttocks of the women...[7]

Whatever the settlers may have thought about the physical features of San people, the San were in some respects superior to them. They could compete with the best painters in the world including those who produced the marvels of Altimore. The San were also unique story-tellers and had the great capacity to dance. This is not all. Rev. Ellenberger quotes Dr. G. Theal as saying of the San,

> They could make their way, in a straight line, to any place
> where they had been before. Even a child of nine or ten years
> of age, removed from its parents to a distance of over a hun-
> dred miles, and without opportunity of observing the features of
> the country traversed, could, months later return unerringly.[8]

In the Cape Peninsula, Jan van Riebeeck is said to have met three Khoi tribes. They kept large heads of cattle and flock of sheep. But in 1653 there is a record that the Khoi people 'stole' forty head of cattle belonging to the Dutch East India Company. As a result of this 'theft' an armed party under a corporal was sent to recapture these cattle by force if necessary.

This stealing of cattle by the Khoi people is puzzling. How could people who had more cattle steal from those who had none? The Dutch East India Company was always struggling to get cattle from the Khoi people. There was a hard fight against the scarcity of food in the Cape Peninsula by the Company. For instance, in 1657 Jan van Riebeeck sent his men out to persuade the Khoi living far afield to sell cattle to the Company. They were also to bring some of their people to the refresh-ment station probably as workers of the Company to overcome the shor-tage of labour which was also a problem for the Company. Jan van

Riebeeck is said to have told his men, 'You must try every imaginable means to persuade them to come to fort or at least to send some of their people.'[9]

There is reason to believe that the stealing of Jan van Riebeeck's cattle by the Khoi was untrue. It is known that as early as 1654 Jan van Riebeeck had discouraged 'private' trade between the Khoi and Company workers. He had forbidden this trade because the buying of ivory, ostrich eggs and such other things, distracted the Khoi from the coveted trade of their cattle with the Dutch East India Company. Without the Khoi cattle the Company had little or no supply of meat.

It is not surprising therefore that exactly seven years after Jan van Riebeeck landed on the southern tip of Africa, another fierce war broke out between the Khoi and the Boer settlers. The Khoi were tired of always having their cattle taken away from them under the pretext that they had 'stolen' them from the Company. A Company that eventually became bankrupt! So the Khoi decided to fight again. But their inferior weapons finally defeated them for the settlers were armed with guns. Many Khoi around the Cape Peninsula became 'detribalized.' They were later tricked into joining the settlers in their wars against another indigenous group. This time the San people.

The San People Resist Colonialism and Dispossession

The Hottentots war around the Cape Peninsula in 1659 was not the first between the settlers and the African people. From the very first Jan van Riebeeck was resisted by the Khoi people when it became apparent their territory was threatened. Ellenberger and Macgregor confirm this in their discussion of the 'Invasion of the Korannas,' they write:

> The Korannas were descendants of the Hottentots who lived at the Cape before the appearance of the Portuguese in 1510. On the arrival of the Dutch in 1652, Qora, chief of the Hottentots, was killed in opposing them, and soon afterwards the whole tribe under the orders of Eikomo, his son, left for the north-west.[10]

It would appear that the Khoi people around Capetown were completely crushed by 1687 for they were reported to have been living 'peacefully' with the settlers; they were now labourers working for meagre wages. The San people were then attacked after also being accused of 'stealing' cattle belonging to the Company or to settlers.

By 1770 some Dutch settlers were miles from the original 'refresh-ment station.' In 1771 another war broke out between the San people and the settlers. The San people had begun to retaliate against the set-tlers who had taken large tracts of their hunting land for farming. As a result of this clash, three landrosts were called to Capetown to plan measures against the San. A reward of three pounds was offered for

> every Bushman, Hottentot or Bastaad robber of any sex or age delivered alive at Robben Island, there to serve the Company in chains... The Graaff Reinet turned out too late, but Jan van der Walt of the Koude Bokkeveld and Jonker Afrikaner... did yeoman service killing over 600 Bushmen and taking a few alive. As a reward for all this, Van der Walt was given two farms on the Nieuwveld.[11]

Sometimes for bribes from the settlers, the 'detribalized' Hotten-tots led the settlers to springs of water and fertile land. Once the Boer settlers had discovered these lands and springs it was difficult to per-suade them to return it to the San people. For example, in the 1770s the San put up a determined resistance against the Boer's encroachment into their country. The Boers enlisted the Hottentot's help. In 1774 a joint force of all the commandos in the areas of Piketberg and Eneeuwberg, under Gothfried Opperman, were sent by the Dutch East India Company representative to search for the San people. A force of 250 soldiers and Hottentot auxilliaries covered a distance of 300 miles. The joint commando force lost one man but it killed over 500 Bushmen and captured 239.[12]

Who Exterminated the Khoisan People?

Gerrit Hanrick, holds the view that the Khoi and San people gradually became extinct during the 18th century. He puts forward as causes for this, indigenous people's susceptibility to European sickness such as smallpox and venereal diseases. Hanrick also reveals that the movement of the whites was characterized by the destruction of the San and Khoi social structures, considerable extermination of the San, and amalgama-tion of the Khoi in the form of a clientship into a European dominated society.[13]

Hanrick also suggests that the expansion of the Xhosa Africans was accompanied by violence against the Khoisan people. It is however, doubtful whether this violence was of the magnitude that could lead to extermination. We have already pointed out that the Xhosa Africans lived peacefully with the Khoi people for many years, intermarriage was common, the Khoi influenced the Xhosa religion and a number of Khoi traditional doctors lived among the Xhosas. This indicates harmonious relations between the Xhosa and Khoi Africans.

The Xhosa Africans were a majority in relation to the Khoisan people. Everywhere the majority would rather absorb the minority population into its own society. A clear example in African history of this is that of the Swazis who mined iron as early as 500 A.D. Communities like those of Maseko, Gamede, Sukati and Magagula, were originally Pedis. But they were absorbed into the Dlamini tribe which was a nucleus of the present Swazi nation. Only extremists in Europe like Adolf Hitler have tried to exterminate the minority—the Jews.

In Africa even Shaka, who was an exception as Napoleon Bonaparte was, cannot be said to have exterminated minority communities. Although he carried out mass killings, unprecedented in the history of Southern Africa. Shaka was an exception: he was the head of a military regime dedicated to unification of African communities and military governments everywhere are often more ruthless than civilian governments.

The Xhosa Africans could not have carried out extermination campaigns against the Khoisan people for like other Africans they believed in the philosophy that a man who 'ate his men' would soon be left with nobody to rule. Persecuted people or those in danger of being exterminated would flee to benevolent chiefs and seek political asylum there. This weakened the power of the 'deserted' chief or tribe.

Jan van Riebeeck and his settler colleagues exterminated teh Khoisan. Ellenberger and Macgregor pointed out that the Boers waged a war of extermination against the Bushmen towards the end of the 18th century.[14]

European colonial records confirm the fact that it was the White settlers in South Africa who exterminated the San people. 'The race is to be entirely subdued or destroyed,' Baron Joachim van Plettenberg instructed colonial governor, Gothfreid Opperman in 1774. Peter Dreyer comments:

> Opperman did his brutal best, as did those who came after him. It was on genocidal expeditions such as these, that the Commando system characteristic of Boer military power was developed—and Boer racial attitudes along with it.[15]

Another historian writes,

> The colonialists turned their attention following the Khoi defeat
> of the San, the settlers adopted a policy of physical extermina-
> tion. Hundreds of San were hunted down and slaughtered, the
> massacres particularly becoming intense after 1715. Some of
> the surviving San children were captured and made slaves...[16]

The few San that survived the slaughter had to flee to the Kalahari Desert
to escape complete annihilation of their entire people by the Boer settlers. The San descendants are today found in Namibia and Botswana.

It must also be pointed out that European settlers never brought
'civilization' to Azania. They brought 'syphilisation'. It was diseases
such as syphilis which helped exterminate the San and the Khoi people.
Africans were reduced in numbers not only through the guns of the settlers, but by the diseases of the settlers brought with them from Europe:
such diseases as dysentry, mumps, influenza, measles and syphilis. But
the greatest killer was smallpox which was introduced into the settlement by a passing ship in 1713.

The disease decimated the Khoisan.

> Whole tribes were engulfed by the disease so that even their
> names were forgotten. Cursing the whites for bewitching them,
> the Khoikhoi fled into the interior to escape. New smallpox
> epidemics struck in 1755 and 1767, and henceforth the
> Khoikhoi were reduced to a landless proletariat—labourers or
> vagrants on the land of their ancestors.[17]

The Khoi alone numbered about 250,000 at the time of the Dutch
settlers. They had trading links with the Batswana in the north whom
they called the *Poricqua* (goat people).'

During the San wars of resistance in the 1770s when they were driven
by the settlers to the mountains, some white settlers were killed. The
settlers became more determined to wipe out the 'little man.' In 1772
for instance, several San people were killed and many taken prisoner.
At the Castle they were either hanged, had their legs broken at the wheel
or had their ankle-sinews cut so that they could serve their life
sentence.[18]

One historian who does not appreciate the fact that the San people
had every right to defend their motherland against the aggressors, and
believed settler stories about Bushmen 'stealing' their cattle, comments:

> It was a horrid, inclusive business. The white men exasperated
> of the raids on their cattle and the sniping of isolated

fellow-burghers by a treacherous foe, hunted the Bushmen down with Hottentots trackers and virtually enslaved their prisoners; the Bushmen, utterly unable to adapt their style of life to changed conditions, desperately defended their hunting grounds.'[19]

Although white historians often describe the San people as the 'little man' of the Stone Age, this little man had big ideas about freedom, liberty and independence. He knew his rights and was always prepared to lay down his life when his God-given gift of liberty was threatened. As one writer puts it: 'They had passionate love for liberty.' He continues, 'They were also very loyal to their chiefs. They showed the greatest devotion and bravery in their attempts to rescue their fellows from slavery—a state which they held in greater horror than death itself.'[20]

How Civilized were Jan van Riebeeck's People?

Jan van Riebeeck and the Dutch East India Company were to profit by any means. Jan van Riebeeck and his colleagues, like Coen, not only broke instructions given to them from Holland, but did anything they felt was in their interest. For example, Jan van Riebeeck allowed his men to marry the Khoi women. Of course, his descendants later legislated against this by their Immorality Act of 1927.

These writers who claim the Boers brought civilization with them equate aggression and invasion by settlers against the indigenous people with 'Western Christian Civilization'. The truth is that the torch-bearers of this 'civilization' had reverted to barbarism. It is true that the settlers could recite long passages of Scripture. They are reputed to have known the Book of Psalms by heart. But their behaviour shows that they did not understand the meaning of what they had memorized. The bulk of these people were the element of settlers which had left the original settlement at the 'refreshment station'. They had fled from the settler-organized state in the Cape Peninsula and were kind of anarchists. No wonder they fought everybody they met and their path was stained with the blood of the indigenous people whom they dispossessed. In some cases as we have seen it was outright extermination.

In case some people are tempted to think that this is the wild imagination of the writer let us quote Walker who himself has quoted various sources showing what kind of people the settlers who caused so much trouble to the indigenous people were.

Hollander visitors complained that they (settlers carrying the civilizing mission) had begun to lose cohesion and cleanliness of home Dutch; a little later de Mist (the settler governor), conning masses of reports from the Company's officials and others, concluded that the extreme frontiersmen, these half-wild Europeans, rebellious and unreasonable in their behaviour were suffering from ' a complete corruption of their moral sense,' a corruption bred by the long distances, from Capetown... the lack of social intercourse with civilized individuals; the monotonous life of herdsmen... the daily hunt, the continual diet of meat... the war... conducted for years against the Bushmen and Kaffirs, a war in which some of them had learnt to doubt whether it really were a crime to kill a native.[21]

References:

1. Peter Dreyer, *MARTYRS AND FANATICS, South Africa and Human Destiny*, p. 70.
2. Eric A. Walker, *A History of Southern Africa*, p. 37.
3. *Ibid.*, p. 37-38.
4. *Ibid.*, p. 30.
5. *Ibid.*.
6. *Ibid.*, p. 33.
7. *Ibid.*
8. D.E. Ellenberger and J.C. Macgregor, *History of the Basuto—Ancient and Modern*, p. 7.
9. Eric A. Walker, *Op. Cit.*, p. 41.
10. D.E. Ellenberger and J.C. Macgregor, *History of the Basuto—Ancient and Modern*, p. 212.
11. Eric A. Walker, *A History of Southern Africa*, p. 118.
12. *Ibid.*, p. 97.
13. Leonard Thompson (ed.), *African Societies in Southern Africa*, p. 146.
14. D.E. Ellenberger and J.C. Macgregor, *History of the Basuto—Ancient and Modern*, p. 212.
15. Peter Dreyer, *MARTYRS AND FANATICS: South Africa and Human Destiny*, p. 63.
16. Ernest Harsh, *SOUTH AFRICA White Rule Black Revolt*, p. 181.
17. Peter Dreyer, *MARTYRS AND FANATICS South Africa and Human Destiny*, p. 97.
18. Eric A. Walker, *A History of Southern Africa*, p. 97.
19. *Ibid.*

20. D.E. Ellenberger and J.C. Macgregor, *A History of the Basuto—Ancient and Modern*, p. 7.
21. Eric A. Walker, *A History of Southern Africa*, p. 99.

5. European Invasion of Azania

In 1689 Simon van der Stel a settler governor who had replaced Jan van Riebeeck sent the Noord captained by Timmerman to the Coast of Natal. Simon van der Stel had ordered him to 'buy' the Bay of Natal. Simon van der Stel had been told that Natal was fertile, possessed a healthy climate and that the natives were industrious and courteous. Timber and ivory was also available from Natal for the Dutch settlers at the Cape. Van der Stel had also gathered from the sailors, that Natal Africans planted crops such as pumpkins, watermelons, calabashes, ground nuts and figs.[1]

This was very tempting for van der Stel. He wanted some land purchased from the Africans there. This contrasts with the view of Azania as an 'empty country' when it was 'occupied' put forward by men like Louw, Verwoerd, and many white historians and apartheid-spokesmen. Some of them even said that only wild animals roamed the country when they took it over.

As the governor had no money how would van der Stel buy this land from Africans in Natal? The Dutch East India Company was on the verge of bankruptcy. As the settlers were unscrupulous, lack of money was no hindrance. Simon van der Stel gave orders to Captain Timmerman to purchase the Bay of Natal and the surrounding territory from a local chief with beads, copper and ironmongery; but he was to take great care that articles of merchandise which represented the purchase price were not enumerated in the document and the price stated in the most general terms. Something like 19 to 20,000 guilders.[2]

Timmerman carried out these instructions to the letter. While the 'agreement' implied the purchase price was 20,000 guilders the chief who 'sold' the land to Timmerman actually received goods worth less than 1,000 guilders. Commenting on this 'transaction', Mackeurtan claims that the African chief 'was incapable of grasping the conception of either the ownership of land or its alienation in perpetuity.

All he intended was to acquiesce in these strange pale gentlemen coming to the Port'.[3]

King Shaka of the Zulus

King Shaka was the last African King to rule a free Natal for he died before the country was taken by force from his half-brother King Dingane. He died in 1828, aged 38, ten years before the Boer trekkers invaded Natal and took it from the Zulus.

It was during the reign of Shaka that the pre-colonial Azania had its peace disturbed by wars among the Africans themselves. These wars, variously called 'Lifaqane' or 'Imfecane', it would seem were basically wars of unification. These wars are often used by Europeans to prove that the white man brought 'civilization' to South Africa. Of course, the truth is that Shaka, a contemporary of France's Napoleon Bonaparte, did in Southern Africa what Napoleon did in Europe. Some Europeans have called Shaka, 'Black Napoleon', while Africans have called Napoleon, 'White Shaka'. In Europe worse men have arisen such as Hitler and Mussolini.

When Shaka ruled a free and independent Natal the whites had already arrived in Azania. There were many traders, mainly of British and American stock, at Port Natal with whom Shaka maintained good relations as long as they obeyed the laws of the country. One of his interpreters, was a white man called Jacob, who was also made a minor chief and commander of one of the regiments. Jacob was very loyal and later hinted to Dingane that the Africans in the Cape Province were being dispossessed of their land by the European colonialists. He warned Dingane to be wary of the movements of Europeans in his country.

Dukuza, now called Stanger was Shaka's seat of government. He also had an important military station at Khangel' aMakengana near what is today called the Bluff and King Edward VIII Hospital in Durban. The purpose of the station was to watch invaders or enemy vagabonds advancing from the sea.

In 1822 Fyn and his brother Farewell left Capetown on a business trip for Natal. It was during this business trip that they tried to 'buy' some land from King Shaka. It is difficult to imagine how an African ruler could sell land: African land was entrusted to the King or his agent—chief or induna; the land was communally owned; the concept of private ownership of land was a totally alien concept. It is therefore puzzling that European writers should say some African rulers 'sold' land to white settlers.

Nevertheless Fyn and Farewell are said to have bought Port Natal and part of the surrounding land from King Shaka. The King is supposed to have signed the following agreement:

> I, Inguos Chaka, King of Zulus and of the country of Natal, as well as the whole of the land from Natal to Delagoa Bay, which I have inherited from my father, for myself and heirs, do hereby, on the seventh day of August, in the year of our Lord eighteen hundred and twenty four, in the presence of my chiefs, and of my own free will, and in consideration of diverse goods received, grant, make over, and sell unto Farewell and Company, the entire and full possession in perpetuity to themselves, heirs, and executors, of the Port or Harbour of Natal, known by the native name of *'Bubolongo'*, together with the islands therein and surrounding country, and herein described, viz. The whole of the neck of land or peninsula in the south entrance, and all the country ten miles to the southern side of Port Natal, together with all the country inland as far as the nation called by the Zulus *'Gokagnekos'*, extending about one hundred miles backward from the sea-shore, with all rights to the rivers, woods, mines, and articles of all denominations contained therein, the said land and appurtenances to be from this date for the sole use of the said Farewell and Company, their heirs and executors, and to be by them disposed of in any manner they think best calculated for their interests, free from any molestation or hindrance from myself or subjects. In witness whereof, I have placed my hand, being fully aware that the so-doing is intended to bind me to all the articles and conditions that I, of my own free will and consent, do hereby, in the presence of the under-mentioned witnesses, acknowledge to have fully consented and agreed to on behalf of F.G. Farewell as aforesaid, and perfectly explained to me by interpreter, Clambermarnze, and in the presence of two interpreters, Coliat and Frederic, before the said Farewell, whom I hereby acknowledge as the Chief of the said country, with full power and authority over such natives that like to remain there after this public grant, promising to supply him with cattle and corn, when required, sufficient for his consumption, as a reward for his kind attention to me in illness from a wound.

Chaka, his X mark
Native Witnesses:
Umbequarn (Chaka's Uncle) his X mark
Umsega, his X mark
Eunclope, his X mark
Clambermarnze (King's Interpreter, his X mark)[62]

According to Mackeurtan, a certificate was attached at the foot of this 'agreement'. It was signed by N.H. Davis, Fyn, Henry Ogle, and one Zinke. Joseph Powell, one of Farewell's men was also a party to this document. Powell was only able to make his mark. And Mackeurtan points out, 'He therefore hardly increased the evidentiary rules of this document with any legal significance.'[5] The land purchased from King Shaka by Farewell according to this questionable document and 'agreement' was 3,500 square miles.

Could Shaka who wanted to bring every king in Azania under his own authority have acknowledged Farewell 'as the Chief of the said country, with full power and authority over such natives that like to remain there ... '? The whole wording of the 'agreement' reflects a Western capitalist mentality not the African concept of communal ownership of land. It is very doubtful that Shaka could have agreed to sell land to Farewell in perpetuity. Indeed, were he alive today Shaka would with regard to the false document he is said to have signed plead non est factum ('that is not my deed').

It is significant that a year after the death of Shaka in 1829, Farewell was killed by an undisclosed 'native chief'. Farewell must have tried to take over land 'bought' from Shaka and the 'native chief' regarding him as an aggressor or worse ordered him to be killed. In African society land could never be sold; it belongs both to the living and the dead. It could be allocated for private use but not for private ownership.

Another interesting aspect about the letter Shaka is alleged to have signed is that witnesses did not give their surnames. For instance, who was Umsega? It does not sound like a Zulu name. Shaka's uncle could not have been Umbequarn for there is no such name in Zulu, nor Euntclope. Legally it would be difficult to identify these people. The only witness who can be traced is Shaka's interpreter, Clambermarnze. He was John Jacob, but the Zulu Africans called him Hlambamanzi (one who came over the waters) presumably a reference to the fact that he had arrived by sea. He had been made a minor chief and commander of one of Shaka's regiments and was married to Zulu women. As he probably knew how to write, it is difficult to understand why he did not sign the document but placed an X mark. This is all the more puzzling as the other Europeans witnessing for Farewell, except Joseph Powell, signed.

Shaka had been impressed by stories he had been told by English traders at the Port about their king. He wanted to establish relations with the English king to whom he referred as 'my brother'. He even tried to send a delegation to England. It was for this purpose he signed the following letter:

> I, Chaka, King of the Zulus do in presence of my principal chiefs now assembled, hereby appoint and direct my friend James Saunders King, to take under his charge and protection Sotobi, one of my principal chiefs, whom I now create of the 'Tugusa' Kraal, Kati my body servant, Jacob my interpreter, and suite. I desire him to convey them to His Majesty King George's dominions, to represent that I send them on a friendly mission to King George ... I require my friend King to pay every attention to the comforts of my people entrusted to his care, and solemnly enjoin him to return them in safety to me, and report to me faithfully such accounts as they may receive from King George ...

John Jacob and N. J. Isaac asked King Shaka to put the X mark as signature to his letter. He refused. Instead he scribbled all over the paper—saying that as he was a great King he must make the greatest show![6]

A signature to this letter to the King of England has never been produced. But a letter in which Shaka was 'selling' land to Farewell with an X mark which cannot be proved to be Shaka's has been kept in colonialists' national archives. Yet the letter to King George seemed more valid than the one involving the 'sale' of land to a private trader. When, however, it is noted that forged documents were used as clever tricks to 'legalize' the dispossession of the African people; it immediately becomes clear why an illegal document is held more improtant than a legal one. At least from the point of view of a valid signature.

The Land-Grabbing Boer Trek

The Boer Trek was the most land-grabbing movement by foreigners in Azania. It is important to remember that in 1652 the Europeans 'owned' a small piece of land as a 'provision station' in Capetown under Jan van Riebeeck. But even this small piece of land was contested by the Khoisan people in their wars of resistance against aggression and invasion. As the Boers began to spread in the Cape Colony itself, taking land for farms, there were wars between them and the Xhosa Africans. But until 1836, Natal, the Transvaal and the Orange Free State provinces of today's South Africa were still under the control and rule of the indigenous Black people.

A number of changes had occurred in the Cape Colony prior to the Boer trek in 1836. In 1795 the Cape had come under British colonial rule but returned to Holland at the Peace of Amiens, in 1802. During the Napoleonic war in 1806 the Cape again fell into British hands. This position remained so until Britain after ruling the whole of South Africa as a colony granted 'independence' to the white minority settlers in 1926.

Ten thousand people were involved in the Boer trek, it is claimed, which took place between 1836 and 1854. Its chief leaders were Piet Retief, Andries Pretorius, Gert Maritz and Louis Trichard. It took place while the Cape colony was under British rule.

The British colonial government was opposed to the ever increasing penetration of the Boers into the interior of the Cape colony because of the armed resistance this action provoked from the indigenous Xhosa Africans, which was costly to the colonial purse. There were times when it cost the colonial government as much as £2,000,000 to put down an uprising by the African people in the Cape. It is also likely that the Cape colonial government was against the Boer penetration because of pressure by philanthropists in England at that time. The British colonial government also upheld equality between the Black indigenous people and the white settlers. They had already abolished slavery in the Cape colony.

The Boers owned several slaves, believing themselves 'superior' to all dark and brown people, they refused to entertain any ideas of racial equality. The Boers believed that Africans were cursed descendants of Ham. The only relationship they could have with Africans, therefore, could only be that of master and servant. Racial equality to the Boers was therefore immoral. To escape the 'absurd' idea of racial equality they determined to go and establish governments of their own where the lot of the blackman in his own land would be oppression, humiliation, as well as the loss land and political power.

Fieldcornet Buchner is on record as saying, 'the uncontrolled behaviour of the Black here is contrary to the care of the Afrikaner sentiment, and that alone is the motivating cause of the migration ... ' Piet

Retief put it more bluntly in his manifesto published just before the trek started in 1836. He said:

> We quit this colony, under the full assurance that the English Government... will allow us to govern ourselves without interference... We are resolved that we will uphold the just principles of liberty; but whilst we will take care that no one shall be held in the state of slavery; it is our determination to maintain such regulations as may suppress crime and preserve proper relations between master and servant...

It is not surprising therefore that the trekkers path in every part of South Africa was marked with bloodshed, land-robbery, military and political suppression of the indigenous African people.

This hated word apartheid was first coined by Prime Minister Daniel F. Malan in 1948. By apartheid he meant to stress on behalf of the descendants of Jan van Riebeeck and the Boer trekkers that Africans could never hope to enjoy any rights in the land in which the Boer trekkers had dispossessed them.

Speaking of the great trek, J. A. Williamson says, Natal was attractive to the 10,000 Boers who had left the Cape in 1836, 'but for the Boers it had two problems. In the north were the homelands of the Zulus, ruled by their King Dingaan. On the coast of Port Natal (afterwards named Durban) there was a little unofficial settlement of British traders, one or two missionaries, and a few Americans. These people dwelt there by favour of Dingane, who was developing a taste for firearms, and had had no recognition from the British government.'[7]

Because the country into which the Boer trekkers were moving, was not 'empty land' and 'only roaming wild animals' as apartheid historians and politicians have suggested, the trekkers went northwards. They could not trek eastward because of the dangers of the 'mountainous country which teemed with natives.' Significantly the Boers trekked in groups so as 'to be better able to withstand attacks by the Bantu.' It would seem that they knew that their actions of land grabbing would be resisted by the Africans, no matter how weak the assegai would prove against the gun.

With the help of the Batlokoa people of Chief Sekonyela the Boers found their way into Natal. However, they stopped at Thaba Nchu in the todays' Orange Free State, where they were well received by Chief Moroka of the Barolong who had previously allowed missionaries to work in his country. It was on the banks of the Vet River that the trekkers began to disagree: some wanted to go to the Transvaal while others, led by Piet Retief, wanted to occupy Natal. Those in favour of the Transvaal pointed out that this part of Azania was further from the Cape colony government. They said that in Natal it was necessary to contend with the Zulus and the British colonial government which was also interested in Natal.[8]

Finally, a few trekkers went to the Transvaal while those under Retief and Maritz went to Natal. They were intent on grabbing any land from Africans they could find. According to their interpretation of the Scriptures it was they the 'meek Christians' who were to inherit the land. They believed that the Africans were the children of Ham and must therefore be treated as men hated by God. The trekkers were armed not only with a dangerous rascist ideology, they had over a thousand wagons and enough guns and gunpowder to put down any assegai resistance by the indigenous Africans.

Of Natal, Piet Retief had said: 'From the heights of these mountains I saw this beautiful land, the most beautiful I've seen in Africa.'[9] In 1837 Retief and his followers reached Port Natal. They were warmly received by the English traders there for this additional strengthening of numbers, improved their 'security' against the Zulu Africans under Dingane. However, the English traders were uneasy about the possibility of Natal coming under the control of a non-British government, but they were a lesser evil than the continued rule of Dingane, and supplied Retief with information on the Zulus.

Without wasting any time, Piet Retief sent a message in October 1837 to Dingane telling him that he wanted to visit him in Umngungundlovu (Dingane's Royal Palace and seat of the then Zulu African Government) to discuss the question of land.

White historians say that after this meeting between Dingane and Retief, the African king accused the Boer trekkers of stealing his cattle. But the trekkers denied this saying that it was Sekonyela the chief of the Batlokoa who had stolen the cattle. The Boers did not say why they had not reported this to Dingane before nor did they say how they knew this. It is said that Dingane then ordered that the cattle be recovered for him from Sekonyela, after which he would give them land. Why Dingane could not have punished Sekonyela by sending his own Zulu army is never explained.

Nonetheless, it must be noted that Sekonyela was the man with whom the Boers had negotiated their passage through Sekonyela's land into Natal. In September 1837 Dingane had received an urgent message which said that a group of 'strange' men riding horses and carrying guns, had come form the Drankensberg mountain and raided the King's cattle.

The Boer trekkers had passed through the Drakensberg mountain into Natal; and no Africans could have been armed with guns at this time, let alone riding horses. The Basotho of Moshoeshoe, for instance, fought with guns much later and used horses only after several clashes, in their wars of resistance against the Boers. These 'strange' men carrying guns could not have been Sekonyela's people, 'strange' men in this context were always understood to be whites. Writing about this episode, T. V. Bulpin says,

> A grandson of Jobe, named Kentethe, had been shot dead and the herdsmen driven away. They had informed Jobe that the raiders had constantly shouted that they were Maboela (Boers). Jobe's son, Sandlovu had tracked the raiders back up the passes of the Mosuthu chief Sekonyela.[10]

It is strange that Sandlovu did not demand those who told him the story to help him capture these dangerous armed thieves. We are told that somehow Dingane believed this story and sent Retief to recapture the cattle 'stolen' by Sekonyela. And it is interesting to note that 'Retief remained at camp until 24 December, while reinforcements poured down the Drakensberg.' These reinforcements came from the same source—Drakensberg, where a force of 'strange men' carrying guns and riding horses had come.[11] Perhaps this was just an unfortunate coincidence, but it did not save Sekonyela who had been so kind to the Boers. To satisfy their insatiable greed for land the Boers were prepared to trick Sekonyela despite his helpfulness.

The trekkers under Piet Retief drove to Sekonyela's place on Christmas eve 1837. One would expect those 'meek Christians' not to do what they did to Sekonyela on the eve of such a sacred day in the Christian world.

> Pretending to have to see him (Sekonyela) again, they returned to his lands, and met him in the garden of the missionary there, the Reverend Allison. Daniel Bezuidenhout (a member of the trekker group) walked up to the chief and produced a pair of handcuffs. He offered to show the chief how to wear these ornaments—and Sekonyela found himself a prisoner.[12]

The trekkers are said to have questioned their prisoner about the stolen cattle. Sekonyela was released after he had 'confessed' that he had stolen Dingane's cattle. The trekkers forced Sekonyela to surrender the stolen cattle, but it is not clear whether they gave these cattle to Dingane or not.

European historians are quick to paint Dingane as an ungrateful savage who punished the Boer trekkers after they had captured the stolen cattle from Sekonyela for him. It is said he tricked the Boers into watching an African Zulu dance. At the dance he suddenly shouted: 'Kill the wizards!' And his men wiped out Piet Retief and his group and went to raid all settlements where the Boers could be found in the King's country.

Daniel Bezuidenhout the Boer trekker who had handcuffed Sekonyela gives the following account of what happened on the night Retief and his men were killed by Dingane's army.

It was about one o'clock in the night, and there was no moonlight. Our camp stood on a rough hillock, nearer the thorn trees. We had three or four bold dogs, that would tear a leopard to pieces without difficulty. I heard the dogs bark and fight, and thought that there was a leopard.

I got up, having no clothes on my person except a shirt and drawers, and went to urge on the dogs: and when I was about three hundred yards from the wagons I heard the whirr of assegais and shields, and perceived we had to do with Kaffirs, not leopards...

I shouted to my brother, 'There are Kaffirs here, and are stabbing the dogs,' and I ran back towards the wagons to get my gun, for I was unarmed. But the wagons were already encircled by three rows of Kaffirs. Still I strove to push with my hands, and struggle, in order to pass through the Kaffirs to get at my gun.

When I had in this way got through the three lines of Kaffirs, rounding the wagons. As I was still advancing I heard my father say, 'God!' and I knew from the sound that he was suffocated by blood. He had a wound in the gullet, above the breast.

Roel Botha had fired three shots, and there lay three Kaffirs, struck down by shots: then, he too, cried 'Oh Lord!' I heard no more, and then I tried to make my way back from the wagons, through the three rows of Kaffirs. Then I received the first wound from an assegai on the knot of the shoulders, through the breast and along the ribs.

A second assegai struck the bone of my thigh, so that the point of the blade was bent, as I found afterwards when I drew it out. The third struck above the left knee—all the wounds were on my left side. A fourth wound was inflicted above the ankle ... I heard no further sound of a voice—all were dead; and the Kaffirs were busy, tearing the tents, and breaking the wagons, and stabbing to death the dogs and poultry.[13]

This account indicates that the Africans understood the intentions of the trekkers to rob them of their land and political rule. They fought bravely with their weak assegais. If they had succeeded, there would have been no monster called apartheid today in their land.

The Boer Trekkers in the Transvaal

Piet Retief was dead, but the trekkers were not going to take this lying down. Re-inforcements came from as far away as the Cape itself. They were now determined to destroy the power of Dingane and possess Natal for themselves.

A group of Boer trekkers under Andries Hendrik Potgieter left the Cape colony in 1835, and were joined by another trekker section under Carel Celliers. The young Paul Kruger who was later to be president of the Transvaal was a member of the latter group. These trekkers passed through the Orange Free State and are said to have been given some land by a Bataung chief called Makwana. The land was between Vet and Vaal Rivers and was 'not very clearly defined.'[14] From there the trekkers entered the Transvaal.

They entered an area of the Transvaal ruled by King Mzilikazi. The trekkers were not only land-hungry, but had dangerous religious beliefs. They therefore, had no respect for any black ruler, and illegally entered Mzilikazi's country. The Matebele were awakened one morning with reports of large number of wagons having entered the country. The Boer trekkers responded rudely when questioned about their movements. Mzilikazi and his people felt insulted, and the Boers were attacked with assegais and several killed.

The Boer trekkers determined to secure African land, re-inforced and in October 1837, declared war on Mzilikazi at Vegkop. It is said they lost two trekkers in this initial battle with the Matebele, but lost all their cattle. After this loss the trekkers went back to the kind Chief

Moroka of the Barolong where they were looked after and given all they needed. At Thaba Nchu, chief Moroka had given permission to Rev J. Archbell to do missionary work. Moroka, however, soon lost most of his land when the trekkers from Graaf Reinet settled in today's Orange Free State and established their government in December 1836. These trekkers were under the leadership of Potgieter and Gert Maritz.

Although the trekkers had defeated Mzilikazi at Vegkop, they felt that this was not enough. All African rulers who resisted the Boer authority were to be completely destroyed. So, Maritz and Potgieter organized an expedition against Mzilikazi. They managed to recruit some Khoi and Barolong people. At Mosega in 1837 at dawn, in a surprise attack, Mzilikazi was defeated and had to flee beyond the Limpopo.

What Kind of Man was Mzilikazi

According to the historian Dr M. C. van Zyl, Europeans found Mzilikazi approachable. He also points out that towards the end of 1835 a small group of American Presbyterian missionaries had actually set up a station near his place at Mosega. Why then did the Boer trekkers attack, drive him from his country and take his land for themselves?

Mzilikazi was an intelligent man, able to distinguish between friendly and hostile whites. He allowed missionaries to do Christian work among his people. Among the Whites with whom he was on friendly terms were men like Robert Schoon and William McLuckie. Before the Boer trekkers disturbed the peace of Azania, Mzilikazi received Sir Andrew Smith the eminent scientist from the Cape colony and gave him the most irreproachable treatment. Smith formed a very high opinion of the Matebele king and he spoke very highly of him to the outside world. Commenting on Sir Andrew Smith's contact with Mzilikazi, Dr. Stanlake Samkange says,

> More important, however, is the disclosure that Mzilikazi contemplated sending indunas to the white King and thus not only reciprocating the Governor's courtesy in sending a message to him through his own ambassador. Thus it came about that, when Smith's party returned to Cape Town, they had with them the first Matebele ever to be sent on a diplomatic mission, Mnombata, the trusted eyes and ears of the Bull Elephant and the Prime Minister of Matebele[15]

On the 3 March 1836 Mzilikazi entered into a Treaty of Agreement with Sir Benjamin D'Urban, representing the British Governor at the Cape colony. In this treaty Mzilikazi undertook among other things to maintain peace, to report movements of people likely to disturb peace in the interior of Azania and to protect all white people who entered his country with his consent. The Cape Governor for his part undertook to forward Mzilikazi's request that the King of England should send a white official to live in Mzilikazi's country.

Of course, the deepest love which Mzilikazi had for Robert Moffat, a white missionary, and the sincere friendship which existed between the two men has no parallel in the history of race relations in southern Africa. Stanlake Samkange in his book *The Origins of Rhodesia* explains Mzilikazi's relationship with Moffat while fighting the white Boer trekkers. He says: 'It is because Moffat had treated Mzilikizi's indunas with respect due to men of their station and rank... ' He continues:

> Most Africans will confess to having a soft spot for a stranger, particularly a white man, who treats them with respect due to them—a fact which might have differently coloured colonial history in Africa if the white man had only grasped it. The indunas must have emphasised to the king the respect and courtesy with which Moffat had received them.[16]

Commenting on the relations which the Boers wanted to have between themselves and the indigenous people of Azania, J. A. Williamson says, 'To the Boers it seemed natural that he should be served by their inferior race. He exacted service with a heavy hand and never had any idea of allowing rights to his subjects.'[17]

References:
1. G. Mackeurtan, *Op. Cit.*, p. 65.
2. *Ibid*, p.66.
3. *Ibid*.
4. *Ibid*, p.106-107.
5. *Ibid*.
6. *Ibid*, p.141-142.
7. *Op. Cit.*, p. 281.
8. T.V. Bulpin, *Op. Cit.*, p. 83.
9. *Ibid*, p.84.
10. *Ibid*, p. 87.
11. *Ibid*.
12. *Ibid*.

13. *Ibid*, p. 88.
14. *Fowler and Smith, History for the Cape Senior Certificate & Matriculation*, p. 282.
15. Stanlake Samkange, *The Origins of Rhodesia*, p. 28.
16. *Ibid*, p. 25.
17. J. A. Williamson, *Op. Cit.*, p. 276.

6. The Battle of Blood River

After the death of Piet Retief the trekkers regrouped and enlisted the support of the English traders and other Europeans from the Cape colony. They fought several battles with King Dingane and his people. Though the Boers were able to drive some Africans from their homes, the Zulu army routed the Boers at every turn. It was in these battles that Boer trekkers like Piet Uys and Dirk Cornerlis were killed. The Zulus were angry at the provocation of Amaboela who had disturbed the peace of their country—Natal. Of the mood of the Zulu army at this time, a missionary wrote,

> About 400 Zulus came bellowing a war song. It sounded exactly like the noise of angry bulls. No one could mistake its meaning. The words were; 'The wild beast (meaning the Boer trekkers) has driven us from our homes; but we will catch him.

A running battle was fought all over the country. The Boer trekkers burnt and killed. At Ndodasuka they burnt the huts and killed all its occupants. Throughout 1838 battle after battle was fought, until the decisive Battle of the Blood River, on the 16 of December, was won by the trekkers.

At this time Mpande, Dingane's half-brother, had sided with the Boers and disclosed several war secrets to them. Of the fierce Battle of Blood River, Daniel Bezuidenhout, the trekker who had hand-cuffed Sekonyela, has said, 'Of that fight nothing remains in my memory except shouting and tumult and lamentation, and a sea of black faces: and a dense smoke that rose straight as a plumbing upwards from the ground.'[1] Carel Celliers another Boer trekker says,

> We were on their right and left, and they were huddled together. We were animated by great courage, and when we had got in front of them, the Kaffirs lay on the ground like pumpkins on a rich soil that had borne a large crop.

When they saw that there would be no escape, as we were driving them towards the sea-cow hole, they jumped into the water and were among the rushes at the river's edge. I believe that all were killed, that not one escaped. I was a witness to the fact that the water looked like a pool of blood: whence came the name Blood River.'[2]

This was a crushing defeat for King Dingane. It was virtually the end of the Zulu power and the loss of their land.

In January 1839 Dingane fled his country and is said to have been killed by 'hostile tribes.' But before he fled Dingane tried to make peace with the Boers. He failed. Mpande the traitor was installed as the Paramount Chief of the Zulus by a leader of the trekkers, Andries Pretorius. Meanwhile the Boers had seized 31,000 head of cattle and over 1,000 Zulu children had been taken as 'apprentices' and distributed among the Boer trekkers. As T.V. Bulpin comments, 'a conveniently camouflaged form of slavery.' In addition to all this, trekkers who had come later than 1838 could have one large farm free.

Natal was not only a 'beautiful country' as Piet Retief had described it, but to the delight of the trekkers, one Cloete found that Natal 'is by far the most healthy part of the country for cattle, and coal is so abundant that in every river of stream the strata lies exposed.'[3]

After the Battle of the Blood River, Dingane sent two of his trusted men with 300 cattle to negotiate peace with the Boer trekkers. Instead of discussing peace with them, Pretorius, the Boer leader arrested the two Zulu warrior diplomats, Ngcobo (whose name was Dambuza) and Khambazana. He conducted a mock trial and sentenced them to death for the murder of Piet Retief. Dambuza argued that he and his colleagues could not be held responsible for the murder of Piet Retief for they had merely carried out their King's orders. However, when Dambuza realised that they were not to be accorded diplomatic immunity, he declared that he was ready to die for his King and people. He asked to be granted two favours: that Khambazana be spared as he was a junior official who had only carried out orders; and that he be killed by 'grown men not boys'.

The Boers rejected both his requests. Instead Pretorius told Dambuza to ask the King above (God) to forgive his sins before he was executed, to which Dambuza announced that he had only one King, Dingane, to whom he would be loyal to the very end. He reasoned that then the King above (God) would surely be merciful to him for faithfully serving his King and people.

Dambuza was then tied to a wagon wheel which was caused to revolve until he was smashed to death.[4] In 1840 the Boers accused Ncapayi, chief of the Bacas of 'stealing' their cattle and marched south of the Umzimvubu to the Kaffir chief, to teach him a lesson. Faku, king of the Pondos and Ncapayi's neighbour was so alarmed by these men armed with guns that he asked for British protection.

The activities of the Boer trekkers in the interior of Azania were even causing some concern among the white people. 'To the British Government, 'writes T.V. Bulpin, *'the whole trek had been a straight-forward act of aggression against the African tribes of the interior...* It seemed to them that it was time to intervene and prevent further bloodshed.'[5] As early as the 14 of November 1838, the colonial governor in the Cape Colony, George Napier had issued a proclamation announcing the seizure of Natal. Declaring Natal a British colony, Napier had said,

> In consequence of the disturbed state of the Native tribes of the territories adjacent to that part arising in a great degree from the unwarranted occupation of parts of those territories by certain emigrants from this colony, being Her Majesty's subjects, and the probability that those disturbances will continue to increase... [6]

Dingane was Finished

Dingane was destroyed. The trekkers had robbed him of his land and throne. Sometime after Piet Retief's death, the trek leader's shooting bag is said to have been found beside his skeleton. In it the Boers are said to have found a document written in English, which was signed by Dingane granting Retief and his trekkers, Port Natal and land from Tugela Umzimvubu, 'and from the sea to the north as far as the land may be useful and in my possession.'[7] The document is said to have been translated for Pretorius by the English adventurer Edward Parker. The document read:

Umkungisloave,

The 4th February, 1938.

Know all men by this that whereas Pieter Retief governor of the Dutch Emigrant South Afrikaans has retaken my Cattle which Sikonyela had stolen which cattle the said Retief now deliver unto me. I, Dingane King of the zoolas do hereby certify

and desire that I thought it fit to resign unto him the said Retief
and his Countrymen on reward of the Case hereabove mentioned,
the Place called Port Natal together with all the Land annexed
that is to say from Dogeela to the Umsoboebo River westward
and from the Sea to the North as far as the Land may be
Useful and in my possession which I did by this and Give unto
them for their Everlasting property.

De merk van		Als getuyge(?)
(Scrawal)		
Koning Dingana		
Als getuijgen(?)		
M.Oosthuisje	(?)Ndona	groot Raadslid
A.C. Greyling	Juliwanco	(illegible)
B.J.Liebeberg	Manondo	(illegible)[8]

This 'agreement' supposedly signed by Dingane giving land to the
trekkers is extremely puzzling and leaves unanswered many questions:
why would such a powerful African king controlling an almost invincible army send strangers to capture cattle for him from Sikonyela
(Sekonyela)? Would Dingane in his normal senses sign a document which
said he was the King of the zoolas? Would he have not asked which people
zoolas were? There never has been such places as Umkungisloave,
Dogeela and Umsoboebo. Dingane would have certainly demanded to
know where these places were. This 'agreement' was written in English,
but the signatures of witnesses and those agreeing to the sale of land
are indicated in Dutch (*e.g. De merk van die Koning Dingane*). Finally
Piet Retief's name does not appear in this agreement'. Retief was the
leader of the Boer trekkers who went into Natal. He led the expedition
against Sekonyela and secured the supposedly stolen cattle. The land was
being 'sold' to Piet Retief, yet he did not sign the 'agreement'. It is more
likely that the alleged agreement was made out after Piet Retief's death
to make a case against the British colonial government, which had its
eyes on Natal. There can be no proof that the alleged X mark found
on this document is that of King Dingane and it is most unlikely that
Dingane would have been party to such an agreement as traditionaly,
land is not sold in African society. Yet despite the suspicious nature of
this document, the 16 of December each year is celebrated by the Boer
descendants in South Africa. The struggle between Dingane and Piet
Retief is seen as a battle between light and 'western christian civilisa-
tion' on one hand and darkness and barbarism on the other.

References:
1. *Op. Cit.*, p. 100.
2. *Ibid*, p. 101.
3. *Ibid*, p. 131.
4. *G. Mackeurtan, Op. Cit.*, p. 257.
5. T. V. Bulpin, *Op. Cit.*, p. 97.
6. *Ibid*.
7. G. Mackeurtan, *Op. Cit.*, p. 245.
8. *Ibid*, p. 245-246.

7. Dingane a Friend of True Civilization

Dingane in fact, was not an enemy of light and true Christian civilization. Missionary work in Natal was established during his reign, and missionaries such as Allen Francis Gardiner and Francis Owen of the Anglican Mission, Aldin Grout, George Champion and Newton Adams of the American Board of Commissioners for Foreign Missions, were welcomed by Dingane in Natal, and their work conducted with his blessing.

There were times when the missionaries angered Dingane but he never molested them nor broke his friendship with them. For instance, Dingane asked Gardiner and Owen to get his army some guns and gun powder. He had heard that Africans in the Cape colony were losing their land to the Europeans and he wanted to prepare his army to defend the country. The missionaries more concerned with souls refused Dingane's request. On so vital an issue of national security another king might have ordered the missionaries death or expulsion; Dingane did neither.

Dingane was keenly interested in education. He asked the American missionaries to establish schools at which his people could learn how to read and write. He promised that even he and his *indunas* (councillors) would attend the school. The advance of the Boer trekkers interupted the plans for the schools and Dingane never had a chance of seeing their establishment. However to Dingane's credit, Adam's College, the famous institution of learning in Natal, resulted from the efforts of missionaries who Dingane had allowed to work in his country. As a result of Dingane's co-operation, a mission station like Groutville was built and therefore indirectly gave South Africa a Chief Luthuli.

Dingane not only had good relations with the missionaries but also with ordinary traders. When he first assumed the responsibility of government, after the death of his brother King Shaka, Dingane assured the English settlers that their security was assured provided they obeyed the laws of the country. The settlers at Port Natal took Dingane at his word and paid several courtesy visits to his palace at Um-ngungundlovu. Some even journeyed from the Cape colonial settlement, to visit Dingane. In 1820 Dr Alexander Cowie and a trader called Benjamin Green visited Dingane. Europeans like Nathaniel Isaac, who left Port Natal during King Shaka's reign, returned to Natal under Dingane's rule and were doing flourishing trade in ivory.

In 1830 Dingane sent John Cane, John Jacob and his *indunas* to the Cape colonial governor to ask the governor at the Cape to facilitate the establishment of diplomatic relations between himself and the king of England. Among other things his message said that he wanted peace with the king of England. He also sent gifts to the Cape colonial government as his token of friendship.

Unfortunately Cane returned hastily to Port Natal, instead of reporting the outcome of his mission to Dingane, where he busied himself with his own commercial affairs. It was left to the other members of the delegation to return and report to Dingane. Dingane was naturally furious with Cane's attitude. He sent a small army to punish him, but Cane disappeared into the bush with some panicking Europeans. Dingane had to send a message to calm the European settlers fears; he told them that it was Cane he wanted to punish, not all Europeans. This appeal calmed the European settlers who all came out hiding. William, Fyn and Henry immediately visited the King to thank him. It is interesting to note that even Cane was forgiven after his traitorous activities.

If Cane had waited until the British Government, through its Cape colonial governor, had replied, diplomatic relations might have been established. This may have prevented the Boer trekkers from moving into Natal; and may have stopped the spread of the national dispossession of the African people and apartheid itself. Unfortunately for both Dingane and the African people, his plans to establish friendly relations with the British Government never materialized

Why did Dingane kill Piet Retief and his Boer trekkers?

Dingane had met and lived with many Europeans; he had chatted with European traders; he had discussed religion with missionaries; he had expressed himself in favour of peace; and had tried to establish diplomatic relations with the English government. In view of this, why then did he kill the Boers?

After the Boers arrival in Natal in 1837, Dingane heard how they had attacked Mzilikazi and driven him beyond the Limpopo River. He had also learned how they had betrayed Sekonyela. African legend has it that Dingane's intelligence service had followed Piet Retief wherever he went without Piet Retief knowing it. It is said that after the Boers had manacled Sekonyela, they had told him exactly what they would do to Dingane the 'heathen king'. Dingane's intelligence service immediately reported all this to Dingane.

Sometime before Piet Retief's death, there had been reports to the *indunas* and the King that people riding 'hornless' cattle had been seen suspiciously encircling the King's Palace at night. On investigation it was found that it was the Boer trekkers who were riding 'hornless' cattle (horses). As they were unable to understand their intentions, the only conclusion Dingane could draw was that the trekkers were spying.

Dingane was constantly reminded of John Jacob's words: he had said that the taking of African land and the overthrowing of of their governments were preceded by the missionaries arrival. Mzilikazi had been with the American missionaries and now he had been overthrown and lost his land. In fact, before the actual killing of Retief and his fellow trekkers, Dingane's indunas had searched Francis Owen for gun powder. Later Dingane personally apologized to Owen for the search.

Dingane was angered by the white traders at Port Natal for they had been running away with African girls. They had also lied to some of Dingane's people. They claimed that Dingane had ordered his subjects near the Port to give cattle to the settlers free of charge. The settlers had also been encouraging African men to go to Port Natal, ostensibly for work, but in actual fact, to recruit them to fight against Dingane and his people. John Cane was known to be raising an army to fight Dingane. In addition to this, Dingane had information that Piet Retief and the trekkers were allies of the English and American traders at Port Natal.

Dingane had tried to supply his army with guns and failed. He was conscious that those who wanted to rob his people of their land had weapons far superior to the assegai his army used. He justifiably feared the Boers. Piet Retief's letter to Dingane merely strengthened his belief that because he was a 'heathen king' he would be destroyed. Piet Retief had said that the great book of God (meaning the Bible) 'teaches us that kings who behave as *Umoslikase* (reference to King Mzilikazi) does, are severely punished, and that they are not allowed to live and reign long.'[1]

Piet Retief arrogantly showed his grey hair to Dingane and told him that he was not dealing with a boy but with a man. The Africans who saw Retief point at his own grey hair and speaking as he did to their king construed this as the most calculated insult and unpardonable rudeness to Dingane and his people. This only mad Dingane more determined to obliterate Piet Retief.

It is significant that when Dingane gave orders he did not say, 'Kill the Europeans!' or 'Kill these White people!' He had met many good Europeans—missionaries, traders and many others. Dingane's order was: *Bulalani abathakathi!* ('Kill the wizards!'). In African society a wizard is: a wicked person; a person who hates; a person who is jealous; a person who covets someone's property; a person who does harm to others without cause. According to Dingane and his people Piet Retief was guilty of all these things. Dingane had not committed any aggression. He had simply defended the country of his forefathers. Dingane's punishment was not aimed at Europeans or white people, but at the wicked covetous land-grabbing Boer trekkers.

In 1840 the Boers complained that the Amabaca Africans had 'stolen' their cattle. They immediately attacked them, recaptured the 'stolen' cattle and killed about forty Africans.[2] This barbarous act so annoyed other white people that Sir George Napier wrote to the Boer trekkers living in Natal saying:

> I can hardly bring myself to believe that men calling themselves Christians, offering up prayers to the Almighty, as the Judge of their conduct and actions, should so profane the holy name of religion as to make a mockery of the word of God, and become the abetter of such cruelty and oppression.[3]

In order to stop further bloodshed in Natal and to maintain order, the British government in the Cape declared Natal a British possession. The Boer trekkers protested bitterly. Their Volksraad (Council) wrote a long memorandum in which they said:

> Immediately after our emigration we declared our in-
> dependence: we established a government of our own: we made
> war upon those who unexpectedly assailed us, and made peace:
> we took possession of unoccupied regions, as well as those that
> we had purchased by our property and blood. The war-craving
> Zulus, by whom we are surrounded, have been checked in their
> hitherto incessant passion for war, so that even now, from fear
> of us, they take up their weapons stealthily and very seldom.
> Two missionaries are already at work amongst them under our

protection: and we have already the best prospects that civilization of that people will advance more rapidly than that of the
Kaffirs on the borders of the Colony (Cape).[4]

In their memorandum to George Napier the Boer trekkers also wrote:

We also disavow most positively that we are animated by an
ingrained hatred towards the English nation. Every man on
earth is naturally more attached to his people than to any other;
but as Christians we have learned to love all men: and although
we, South African Boers, have often been regarded with dis-
dain and contempt by Englishmen, let the many English... bear
witness, let the officers and soldiers with whom we have served
together in arms, bear witness...[5]

References:
1. Fowler and Smith, *Op. Cit.*, p. 287.
2. G. Mackeurtan, *Op. Cit.*, p. 262.
3. *Ibid*, p. 262-263.
4. *Ibid*, p. 266-269.
5. *Ibid*.

8. Moshoeshoe and the Boer Trekkers

In the interior of Azania the Boer trekkers not only found Dingane in Natal and Mzilikazi in Western Transvaal, but African people such as Pedis, Vendas, Hlubis and others in the Transvaal; the Basotho, the Barolong, Batlhaping and others in the Orange Free State. Little or no resistance was offered by some African people in the wake of the trekkers fire power: the Vendas were taken by surprise by Louis Trichard and dispossessed; the Barolong were tricked into surrendering huge tracts of land to the Boer trekkers.

The Barolong believed that the missionaries would never do anything that was against the interests of the indigenous Africans. The Barolong, Chief Moroka, had helped the Boer trekkers and allocated them land to use according to communal usage of land. But the Boers claimed 'ownership' of huge tracts of land. The Barolong decided not to fight; but Moshoeshoe and the Basotho people resisted.

The question of land 'ownership' was the cause of friction between the Basotho and the Boers. The Boer trekkers continued to take possession of the land of the Africans. Moshoeshoe and his people maintained that the land to the Caledon River and to the Vaal River belonged to the Basotho Africans. Some trekkers had settled along the Caledon River with Moshoeshoe's people, but later claimed the land as theirs. A view Moshoeshoe refused to accept. He explained that the land had been granted to the trekkers only for temporary use. The land he claimed was communally owned by the Basotho. There was no 'private ownership' of land in African society. The land in contention did not belong to any single African either. Moshoeshoe pointed out that the land had belonged to his ancestors for many years and that the law governing the use of land could not be changed by whites. In effect he argued the Boer trekkers were his subjects as they had come to his land. The Boer trekkers did not accept this view. And fortunately for them, the British colonial government in the Cape Colony pressurized Moshoeshoe into changing his attitude. The British drew a boundary, the Warden Line, around the land depicting that which was Basotho land and that which 'belonged' to the Boer trekkers. Moshoeshoe and his people refused to recognize this 'boundary', and this sparked off the so-called First Basotho War.

The Basotho people scored a glorious victory in their first war of resistance against Boer aggression. On the 25 April 1858 the Basotho warriors drove the Boer trekkers away. The Basotho Africans had been fortunate for they had managed to acquire some guns. The Boer trekkers left the African land defeated, crying, 'Let us go home.'

It proved a temporary victory for the Basotho. Boshoff, the Boer leader soon won Sir George Grey's support. He 'mediated' between Boshoff and Moshoeshoe and the Treaty of Aliwal North was drawn up. In it Grey had made the boundary line from Caledon as far as the Orange River. The northern point of the Warden Line, the districts of Harrismith and Winburg, were left out and Boer possession conceded.

Moshoeshoe and his people were dissatisfied with Grey's new boundary as the Warden Line. But Moshoeshoe feared that if he resisted the Orange Free State Boer trekkers would unite with the English settlers against him. So Basotho discontent continued to simmer.

Early in 1865 Moshoeshoe ordered his people to reoccupy the districts of Winburg and Harrismith which were occupied by the Boer trekkers. With the aid of guns the Boers were attacked and most of the land was restored to the Basotho Africans. Moshoeshoe had ignored 'boundaries' drawn by aggressors and invaders. The Treaty of Aliwal North was no longer accepted. J.H. Brand, trekkers' leader, appealed to the British government in the Cape. He requested Governor Wodehouse to 'mediate'. The British 'mediator' said that the Warden Line was the 'legal boundary' and declared Moshoeshoe 'guilty' of violating the boundary. The result of this 'mediation' made the Boer trekkers go hysterical with joy. It was just before the harvest when the British mediated in favour of the land-grabbing trekkers. Moshoeshoe decided not to show his dissatisfaction immediately. First the people must harvest their fields and then prepare for war to defend their sacred fatherland. *Tsie e fofa ka mokona* (an army marches on a full stomach).

By May 1865 Moshoeshoe was ready for war. He refused to abandon his land in the districts of Winburg and Harrismith and others. In June 1865 Brand declared war on the Basotho Africans. He had the support of the Transvaal Boer trekkers. But Moshoeshoe defeated the combined armies of the trekkers so ignominiously that 'it looked as though Moshesh had organised all natives in South Africa against the whites,' as as one writer puts it.

Through diplomacy Moshoeshoe had also won the sympathy of the colonial government by convincing the British government that Brand and the trekkers were aggressors. This was no mean achievement on the part of Moshoeshoe as we shall see later when we discuss the role of the British colonial government from 1842 to 1895 and beyond that date.

The Basotho Africans armed with guns, riding horses and having stored plenty of food for the war, fought the Boer trekkers like angry tigers. They chased the Boers from almost every part of their original Lesotho. They penetrated within 30 miles of today's Bloemfontein. This part of the Orange Free State was ruled by Chief Moroka who was a vassal of Moshoeshoe. Boer houses were burnt down and 100,000 sheep captured as punishment for the Boer trespass on the land that was not theirs.

But the Boers were not going to take this lying. In this Second War with the Basotho they were determined to be victorious. Their defeats by the Basotho were merely lost battles. They were determined to win the final war. Commandant Louw Wepner led his troops direct to the stronghold of the Basotho—Thaba Bosiu (mountain at night). Wepner had vowed that his soldiers would capture Moshoeshoe himself and that he (Wepner) would that night sleep with 'Ma—Mohato (Moshoeshoe's senior wife and Queen of the Basotho). Wepner's military campaign against the Basotho at Thaba Bosiu ended disastrously for the Boer aggressors. At the Battle Thababosiu Wepner was speared by Makoanyane (one of the great African warriors) as he was trying to climb the steep mountain. The trekkers fled. This was early in 1865.

The British colonial government's sympathy for the Basotho soon waned, for they were afraid that the Basotho victories against the Boer vagabonds would encourage Africans in Natal and the Cape colony to take up arms and challenge the authority of the English settlers. They made sure that Moshoeshoe received no fire-arms or ammunition while the Boers obtained their weaponry needs. Moshoeshoe's army was gradually forced to rely on the assegai and knob-kerries as weapons. With superior weapons the trekkers soon forced the Basotho to retreat, in April 1866. Trekker commandos harrassed the Basotho until Moshoeshoe was forced to abandon large tracts of fertile wheatlands. This land became known as the 'Conquered Territory'. The Basotho people were left with very little, only the present mountainous Lesotho, completely surrounded by settler South Africa.

In July 1867, the Third Basotho War of Resistance erupted. In an attempt to restore their stolen land the Basotho Africans decided to fight a guerrilla war from the caves and mountains, relying on surprise attacks. They completely avoided pitched battles; their plan was to prolong the war and wear out the Boer trekkers, now entrenched in Basotho land, claiming it as theirs and calling it the Orange Free State after a Dutch prince of Holland. The wars continued for twenty years, until the weight of fire power and the support of the British colonial government the Basotho were finally defeated. 'As the reward of victory the Free Staters not only claimed the disputed territory *but the whole of the agricultural part of Basotholand proper*, leaving the mountains to the Sotho.'[1]

Moshoeshoe on the stolen land and white settlers

When the Boer settlers arrived in the 'Orange Free State', King Moshoeshoe said:

> I have heard previously of the custom of the whites of purchasing and selling lands. I consider it a most abominable and barbarous custom to alienate the property of the tribe (nation) which they hold so sacred. I shall not accept *pego* (money?) from any of you. I only lend you the cow to milk. You could use her, but I will not sell the cow. I allow you to remain, even if it is a year or two that you might rest on your way. *We must warn you that we look upon you merely as passersby*.

In a letter to 'President' Boshof, in later years, Moshoeshoe said, 'we wondered when we saw the whites cross into Senqu (Orange) River (1836). They crossed by lots. They begged from the blacks for pastures everywhere, one by one, in a good soft manner. We did not imagine that they would appropriate the land for themselves. When I heard that they were purchasing farms from each other, I hastened to issue a proclamation (20 October, 1844) telling the whites: 'Do not barter land for it is not the custom of us Basotho to do so'. According to our custom, the land belongs to all the people, it is not disposed of by bargain, and also it is not our habit to define limits in it.'

Moshoeshoe also reflected on the Boer settlers' reasons for warring on the African people. In 1865 Moshoeshoe said 'the grievances of the Boers were no serious reason for war... all people know that my great sin is that I possess a good and fertile country.' While earlier, in

1859, Moshoeshoe had said:

> The white men seem to be bent on proving that in politics Christianity has no part... it may be that you white people do not steal cattle, but you do steal whole countries; and if you had your wish you would send us to pasture our cattle in the clouds.

Criticizing the Boer settlers twisting of truth King Moshoeshoe commented:

> When we drive the Boers' cattle, sheep and horses in war, or before their fearing faces, they call that stealing. When they drive ours, they call it soft names. They say they recapture or replace their stolen ones... To us, capturing the enemies' property in war, is one way of self-protection. *More than that, by us, all the property reared and nurtured on land stolen from us, remains our property.* Are whites not larger thieves, for *they are also stealing black man's land in the (Cape) Colony to here and call it theirs*?[2]

The Bapedi People and the Boer trekkers

The Bapedi Africans put up little resistance to the trekkers' invasion and establishment of the 'South African Republic' in the Transvaal. These Africans weighed their assegais against the guns of the Boers. They realized that whether they fought or not, the trekkers would overthrow their government and seize their land. But many Bapedi Africans of Sekhukhuni had rushed to the mines after the whites discovered diamonds in the Transvaal. Here they managed to illicitly buy fire-arms and ammunition. Once armed, they decided to fight for the return of their land.

Meanwhile Rev T.F. Burghers, the leader of the trekkers in the Transvaal was working to establish a railway line through Delagoa Bay. The proposed railway line was to run through Bapedi land which they had retained despite their losses to the trekkers. In 1876 Burghers launched a pre-emptive attack on the Bapedi ruler, Sekhukhuni, and his people. By this time, the Bapedi Africans were partly armed, and the trekkers suffered a humiliating defeat. As a result of Sekhukhuni's victory over Burghers the Zulus in Natal under Cetywayo threatened to regain their own land in Natal by force. The British colonial government in th Cape feared that the Bapedi victory would lead to armed insurrection by Africans under their rule.

Through their newspapers, *Gold Fields Mercury* and *Transvaal Advocate*, the English-speaking diamond diggers put pressure on the British government to annex the Transvaal. The English became increasingly opposed to the Transvaal Boer republic. Sir Henry Barkley wrote a strong letter to Burghers in which he accused him and his fellow trekkers of land-hunger and of provoking trouble among the natives in the interior of Azania. The British government quickly annexed the Transvaal on the 2nd February 1877. But despite the annexation, Sekhukhuni refused to acknowledge the authority of either the Boers or the British, and rejected their agent Theophilus Shepstone. The British had no option but to fight the Bapedi in order to break Sekhukhuni's authority. He was finally beaten by superior weaponry after twenty months of fighting, at the enormous cost of £300,000.

Waterboer claims land from the trekkers

Everywhere the Boer trekkers went land disputes erupted. Every African community had its land taken by force when necessary. In 1862 a Griqua (Khoi) chief, Cornelius Waterboer, claimed land along the Vaal and Haarts rivers (Campbell Lands). Instead of using military force he engaged a lawyer, Anorld David, and had the matter submitted to arbitration. In 1871 Keats, the arbitrator, gave his considered ruling: the whole of the disputed territory between the Vaal and the Harts rivers belonged to Cornelius Waterboer, a Khoi chief. Encouraged by this result, the Batlhaping people claimed their land from the Boer trekkers in the Orange Free State.

The Boer trekkers say they found Azania uninhabited. The Africans were pastoral farmers it was quite normal to graze cattle in different areas, according to the seasons. It is therefore possible that the Boers on some very rare occasions may have found the African peasant farmers away in either their winter or summer pastures. However, this cannot be construed as 'unoccupied' land. During the *Difaqane* or *Imfecane* (Shaka's wars) some people fled in fear of Shaka and Dingane only to find the trekkers had claimed their land as Boer land.

The fact is that the land which the Boer trekkers occupied was taken from the Africans by force: Dingane's seat of government at Umngungundlovu was burnt down and destroyed after the Battle of Blood River and renamed Pietermaritzburg, in honour of Piet Retief and Gert Maritz; Mizilikazi in Western Transvaal fled across the Limpopo River after his land was taken from his people by the Boer guns; Moshoeshoe lost his land to the Boer trekkers in the Orange Free State.

Several places which had African names have settler names today. The Orange River itself was known as *Senqu* (Sotho) or *iGqili* (Xhosa) by the Africans. It was renamed by the Boer trekkers: Ga Mogale became Witwatersrand; Namahali became Elands River; Noka Tlou became Piet Spruit; and so on.

Rev D.E. Ellenberger of the Paris Evangelical Missionary Society and J.C. Macgregor (British Assistant Commissioner in Leribe, Lesotho in 1910) write in their book, *History of the Basuto Ancient and Modern*:

> Towards the end of the eighteenth century... The Boers waging a war of extermination against the Bushmen, and advancing from Graaff-Reinet more and more to the north, forced the Hottentots beyond the Orange River. Their advanced parties crossed the river at the spot where Hopetown now stands, where they encountered the Batlhaping, whom they reduced to starvation by robbing them of their stock.
>
> Here they were joined by others of their race, called the Springboks, and the most influential man among them was chosen as captain of the whole. This was Jan Bloem, a German by descent, and an evil doer; who, with the aid of his gun, had already enriched himself by seizing the cattle of his neighbours. From Hopetown they resided for a time near a spring, which ever since has borne the name of Bloemfontein, called after this rascal, and where the capital of the Orange Free State was afterwards erected.[3]

The Boer trekkers have continued to take possession of African land. Under the Bantu Settlement Scheme and Group Areas Act, African land can be declared 'white spot' by proclamation and the African has no recourse. This continued suffering was aptly conveyed to a white Anglican priest by a Zulu peasant of Babanango. The spokesman for the Babanango tribe said in 1967:

> Father, we are coming from Babanango. We are suffering and ask you to intercede with the Government for us so that we too may be able to live as people with sensitive souls.
>
> You already know something of this matter since we met with you recently. But we would like to explain to you briefly how things have gone: our ancestors were living in this place at

the time of Senzangakhona, the father of Shaka. Afterwards the place fell into the hands of the white man and we gave allegiance to them. Now we are being expelled.

We do not want to argue with the law but we ask the authorities to sympathise with us in this matter. If we are moved from here we request the Government to find us a place where we will be able to keep cattle and have fields...[4]

References:
1. I. Schapera (Ed.), *The Bantu speaking Tribes of South Africa*, p. 346.
2. Ntsu Mokhehle (Ed.), *Moshoeshoe I Profile*, p. 25-31.
3. D. Ellenberger & J.C. Macgregor, *Op. Cit.*, p. 212.
4. Cosmos Desmond, *The Discarded People*, p. 55

9. The role of Britain in the scramble for Azania

By 1854, although the African wars of resistance were still raging, Azania was now divided into two colonial regions: the Transvaal and the Orange Free State controlled by the Boer settlers; while the English settlers had turned the Cape and Natal into British colonies.

In the Transvaal and Orange Free State, the Boer settlers tried to form a union of the two territories but proved impossible due to internal quarrels and jealousies. In 1857 W.W. Pretorius, a settler president of the South African Republic in the Transvaal, staged a coup d'etat in the Free State, which failed. Pretorius and M.A. Coetz were driven out of the country by Boshoff a settler president of the Orange Free State.

The Boer settlers in the Transvaal and Orange Free State practised a policy of racial inequality. While in the British colonies of Natal an Cape Colony, a sham 'equality' existed. Only Africans deemed 'civilised' qualified for equality with the English settlers. The oppression and humiliation Africans suffered under the rule of Boer settlers was far worse than under the British colonial administration.

The British colonial government had earlier sided with the indigenous Africans when it was in their interests to do so. Later in 1851 their policy changed when their interests changed and the Africans were regarded as enemies. The British pursued a policy of signing 'treaties' with some African rulers while supplying the Boers arms.

In 1851 Moshoeshoe disputed a boundary established under Warden. The British retaliated and sent troops to reinforce their boundary claims; war ensued. The Basotho inflicted a serious defeat upon the colonial troops at the Battle of Viervoet.

This reversal frightened the British colonial government. In 1850 they had battled with the dissatisfied Xhosa Africans in the Cape. The Xhosa Africans were backed by Khoi Africans (Hottentots). This was the eighth war of resistance by the Xhosas. The Xhosas under Sandile had been in communication with Moshoeshoe of the Basotho for a common military strategy against the European invaders. The British colonialists were now afraid that the Africans might unitedly launch a general uprising in a bid to recapture and repossess their land.

British policy toward the Africans swiftly changed. 'The declared object of the Blacks is to drive the White man into the sea,' the English colonial newspaper, *Friend of the Sovereignty* cried. Harry Smith, the colonial governor agreed with the newspaper. In his report to London he wrote: 'There is not a Black man in South Africa, whatever may be his descent, who is not inimical to British rule.'

Warden, who had been ignominiously defeated by the Basotho Africans at the Battle of Viervoet, earlier in the year, said: 'This year 1851 must decide the mastery between the White and Coloured race both here and in the Colony.'

In 1852 the British Government recognised the Boer 'republic' in the Transvaal by signing the Treaty of Sand River. At the Sand River Convention, the British adopted a pro-Boer position. George Cathcart, who had succeeded Harry Smith as the British colonial governor had just defeated the Xhosa Africans in the Eighth War of Resistance. In December 1852, Cathcart's 2,500 soldiers marched into Basotho land to 'subjugate' Moshoeshoe, but at the Battle of Berea, Cathcart's army was ignominiously defeated by the Basotho warriors. This confirmed the British colonialists' wisdom in siding with the Boer settlers. In 1854 the Orange Free State 'republic' was officially recognized at the signing of the Bloemfontein Convention.

This represented a complete reversal in British policy towards the African people. On one occasion the British colonial administration had said: 'These migratory Boers are not to be recognized as one of the regular powers of the world.' But now, the British government had decided that the migratory Boers were a 'regular power' to be recognized.

However, the British colonialists were so inconsistent for, only a few years later, they repealed the Sand River and Blomfontein Conventions and annexed the Transvaal and the Orange Free State—making them part of the British colonies in South Africa at the 1902 Vereeniging Convention.

What was the cause of this change in British policy?

Diamonds had been discovered in the Transvaal. As the Cape Colony's economy was depressed, it was expected that the newly discovered

Transvaal diamonds would produce the needed upturn. In 1868 the British colonial newspaper the *Friend of the Sovereignty* described the Boer republics as a: 'source of ruin and disparagement to colonial merchants, and a heavy stumbling-block to English enterprise and progress on this continent.'

The fear that the newly discovered diamonds would make the two 'republics' stronger than the British colonies of Cape and Natal prompted the British to seek sovereignty. In 1871 the colonial governor in the Cape, Barkly, wrote to London:

> It requires no gift of prophecy to predict that should the Free State be suffered to absorb the best portion of the diamond fields, as seems but too probable, it will soon rival the Eastern and Western provinces in wealth and population, and it will not be then content to play a secondary part, or go on paying customs and duties at the Cape ports... without attempting retaliation.

Clearly the Boer republics were brought under British rule to keep them economically weak and dependant on the British coastal colonies.

As British policy had prevented the Boers from acquiring more land, the trek had commenced in 1836 as the Boers quest for land continued. They 'regarded themselves as resembling the Israelites of old, pushing into promised land and smiting any occupants who stood in their way...'[1]

Williamson added:

> On the Kaffir frontier there were constant disputes between white and black. Cattle stealing was a common cause. When the farmers lost cattle it was customary to form a commando or armed party, ride into Kaffir Land and 'recognize' the stolen beasts. Needless to say, recognition was not always too scrupulously done.[2]

It is often said that the clash between the Xhosa Africans was caused by their stealing of cattle belonging to the Boers. This is not true. The dispute was about the land. The settlers often claimed land belonging to Africans and asked certain 'boundaries' to be observed. In the Cape the Xhosa Africans fought twelve wars of national resistance against the aggression of the Boers and the English settlers. Several settler governors had tried to fix the Fish River as the boundary between the Xhosas and the settlers. But how could the African people be expected to observe

a 'boundary' resulting from the aggression of the settlers?
One colonist wrote of the frontier problems:

> The eastern frontier of the Colony (Cape) had for many years
> been to the governors a burning problem. This area was sparse-
> ly inhabited and farmers were continually exposed to attack
> from the invading Xhosas. The policy of regarding the Fish
> River as a line of segregating the white colonialists and the
> Bantu had been followed consistently by the British authorities
> as a frontier measure since 1806, but no effective military
> measures were taken to safeguard the frontiersmen from Bantu
> raids in the Zuurveld.

When the Earl of Caledon became Governor of the Colony in 1809,
he sent Colonel Collins to inspect the frontiers. Collins advised that the
maintenance of the Fish River as the boundary between the white colonists and the Xhosa Tribes should be continued. The Xhosa should be
driven across the Keiskama and the area between the two rivers unoccupied so that an effective policy of segregation could be maintained.
Moreover, a large white population of small farmers should be settled
in Zuurveld to keep the Xhosas out. He recommended that some 6,000
British colonists should be settled there. This policy could not be immediately effected as Caledon had to avoid excessive military expen-
diture at a time when the Napoleonic Wars had reached a critical stage
in Europe.[3]

Battles won but war lost

In October 1852 George Cathcart gave an ultimatum to Moshoeshoe to
return 1,000 horses and 10,000 'stolen' cattle. With no desire to fight
a war which he might lose, Moshoeshoe, promised to pay 3,500 cattle
and the balance later. When Cathcart rejected this offer, Moshoeshoe
warned him: 'Do not talk of war, even a dog will show its teeth when
provoked. I will do my best to pay you the horses and cattle you want.
I hope that God will help me raise the number you are demanding.'
On the last day of Cathcart's ultimatum the African King handed
over the 3,500 cattle he had promised. Cathcart remained unsatisfied
and ordered 2,500 troops to march into the Basotho land to 'teach the
savage ruler a lesson.' Unperturbed, Moshoeshoe met force with force
at the Battle of Berea, and defeated the British army.
In 1846 the British colonial government sent the colonial soldiers

to attack the Xhosa Africans under Sandile. Despite their lack of guns the Xhosa warriors defeated the British at Burnshill. In 1850 Governor Harry Smith deposed King Sandile because he was 'unco-operative' with the colonial governors. The English missionary Charles Brownlee replaced the African King, but as long as their King lived, the Xhosa Africans refused to have anything to do with him.

When Smith tried to enforce his authority, war broke out when on the 24th December 1850, the Xhosa warriors began to harass Smith's settler soldiers. On the following day the Xhosa Africans 'wiped out three of Smith's costly military villages. In all directions the tribes sprang to arms.'[4]

When the Xhosas scored successive victories against the settlers, the Khoi Africans joined the Xhosas. The 'Kaffir police and even the Coloured Cape Mounted Riflemen went over to the enemy'[5] commented one European writer. This culminated in the Battle of Sandile's Kop which inflicted yet another devastating defeat upon the settlers.

The battle which took place in Natal in 1879 was another victory by the indigenous Africans. After provocation by the settlers, the Zulu Africans, under King Cetywayo fought back. In a surprise attack the Africans killed 1,400 British soldiers, while only 400 escaped. The Battle of Isandlwana as this battle is called, ranks as one of the most humiliating defeats the European settlers suffered in Azania.

About 1881 the indigenous Africans had lost everything—their land, wealth, political power and their national sovereignty and human dignity. They had started a life of unwanted and exploited people in the land of their forefathers.

The union of South Africa

The Transvaal and the Orange Free State became part of the British colonial South Africa in 1902. They had some form of internal government and a 'native policy' of their own. As we have noted earlier, there was a limited franchise in Natal and Cape for Africans, but there was no such right in the Transvaal and Orange Free State where the Boer settlers had earlier established their 'republics'.

The Africans, completely crushed militarily and now virtually under the European colonial rule, were still resisting the colonial rulers. To consolidate their position, the settlers formed the Union of South Africa, consisting of four colonies. It would strengthen the country economically. A union would strengthen the Boer republic of the Transvaal. In the

Transvaal there was no strong central government. W. Pretorius, the Commandant-General of the Boer settlers had had influence and authority only in the districts around Potchefstroom and Rustenburg. The other Boer settler leaders around Zoutpansberg and Lydenberg acted independently. This was one of the reasons the Boer settlers had been defeated by the Bapedi Africans under Sekhukhuni.

But the chief reason the European settlers wanted a Union of South Africa was to consolidate their political position over the Africans they had dispossessed. Writing on the need for a common native policy, Fowler and Smith say:

> Peace in South Africa depended to a large extent on a sound relationship between colonies and the republics on the one hand and the Native tribes adjoining their boundaries on the other. The Transvaal was concerned with the Bapedi and the Swazi; Natal with the powerful Zulus, who were kept on good terms with the colony as a result of masterful control of Shepstone; and the Orange Free State with the Basuto. The Cape Colony was to deal with the warlike Xhosa tribes on its eastern frontier. It was common knowledge to the governments concerned that when one tribe was involved in war, peace was also endangered in other parts of South Africa. *Unified control of the Native tribes in South Africa through some form of federation would minimize* the danger of costly Native wars and maintain peaceful conditions.[6]

The idea of federation had been championed by men like Lord Carnarvon and Sir George Grey. In the Orange Free State many Boer settlers had always been in favour of joining a union of South African colonies under white control. As early as 1858 the Boer settlers in the Orange Free State had a federation with the Cape as 'the best way of ending the Basotho danger.'[7]

In October 1908, a National Convention was convened in Durban to discuss the formation of a Union of South Africa. There were thirty three delegates. The Cape Colony had twelve representatives, the Transvaal eight while Natal and Orange Free State had five each. Southern Rhodesia (Zimbabwe since April 1980) was represented by three observers and had no right to vote 'as that colony had no definite desire to join in a union until its affairs with the Chartered Company had been settled.'[8]

Amongst the prominent delegates at the 'national convention' were men like Smuts, Botha and Fitzpatrick (Transvaal), Merriam, Sauer, Jameson (Cape Colony), Hertzog and Steyn (Free State), and Moor (Natal). The 'national convention' was a 'Europeans only' convention. The indigenous Africans were not represented. How could they be when the 'national convention' was called to work against their interests? In fact, many sessions of this convention were held behind closed doors.

In 1909 the draft constitution of the Union of South Africa was agreed, and referred to various parliaments of the European settlers for ratification. After some amendments by the Cape, Natal and the Orange Free State, the constitution was adopted. However, Natal wanted a referendum to test the popularity of such a union. Natal settlers were suspicious that their province

> would be subjected to Dutch dominance, whereas hitherto it had been almost entirely British. Contrary to general expectation, the referendum, held in June 1909, revealed an overwhelming majority in favour of Union. A delegation then proceeded to London, where the constitution was passed by the British Parliament before the end of the year, in the form of the South Africa Act of 1909. On the 31 May 1910, the Union of South Africa came into being with Louis Botha as the first Prime Minister.[9]

In the light of the South African Government's current apartheid policy to create weak statelets in the form of Bantustans, it is interesting to note the following points:

At the formation of the Union of South Africa some European settler politicians advocated a federation. However Jan Smuts supported by an overwhelming majority of the settlers strongly defended the unitary form of government as against a federal structure. Fowler and Smith put forward the reasons for this when they noted that:

> Many reasons were advanced why union should be accepted. The colonies needed a strong central government in view of the many grave problems that had to be settled. This would be impossible in a federation where the central government was weak, and where the provinces may carry out a policy half-heartedly which might be distasteful to them. Some argued that the federation encouraged corruption, and that a federal constitution was too rigid and might possibly lead to friction between the central and local governments as was the case in

Australia and Canada or even a civil war as the history of the United States had shown. Some, again, maintained that the administrastion in a unitary constitution would be less costly than that of federation.[10]

The Union of South Africa was in the interest of the settlers of Europe, although they had to compromise to achieve it. When deciding the official language—English or Dutch?—it was agreed that both should be official, on an equal footing 'since the two races had agreed to enter the Union on a basis of equality.' A clause, to this effect was written into the Constitution.

The choice of capital provided the next contentious issue. However as a comprise, Capetown became the legislative capital and Pretoria the administrative capital. Bloemfontein on the other hand was made the seat of the Appeal Court.

Finally the vote for the Africans, precipitated a major storm. Men like Sauer in the Cape proposed that there should be a uniform franchise for Africans throughout the Union of South Africa. Sauer recommended the Cape system which had allowed equal rights for *all* British subjects in the Cape Colony. The Boer settlers in the Orange Free State and Transvaal who had left the Cape to establish 'governments' where *proper relations between master and servant* would be observed, rejected this proposal. In their former 'republics' only European settlers had been given the franchise.

Ultimately the Cape proposed that the voting laws be left as they were: that is that the Africans in the Transvaal and Orange Free State should not vote; but that the Africans in the Cape not be deprived of their limited franchise. This was agreed and the voting right of the indigenous Africans in the Cape was made a clause. This meant that it needed a two-thirds majority of members of Parliament of both houses to revoke it. Of course, while Africans in the Cape could vote, they could not become members of parliament. The African franchise itself was a qualified one. Only certain 'advanced natives' could vote. Yet the most-backward Boer settlers in the Transvaal and Orange Free State farms could vote. The Union of South Africa was therefore, an apartheid settler union established on racial discrimination. The British in effect had laid the foundations of apartheid.

Africans opposed to the Union of South Africa

Although, Africans had no voice at the 'national convention' which lay the foundation of the Union of South Africa, they had been concerned by its formation. In the Cape Province, Professor D.D.T. Jabavu, who owned and edited *Imvo Zabantsundu* (African Opinion) opposed the move to deprive the Africans of the vote. He felt that all His Majesty's British subjects regardless of colour should be given the vote. In general, the Africans felt that the bringing in of the Transvaal and the Orange Free State into the union with Natal and Cape Colony would deprive them of advancement as a people.

Wide-spread protests were made by the African spokesmen throughout the country. They complained that the British Government had handed them over to be perpetually oppressed by granting 'independence' to a foreign settler minority government in an African country. As usual the British Government ignored their plea.

References:
1. J.A.Williamson, *Op. Cit.*, p. 276.
2. *Ibid.*, p. 278.
3. Fowler and Smith, *Op. Cit.*, p. 265.
4. Eric A. Walker, *Op. Cit.*, p. 251.
5. *Ibid.*
6. Fowler an Smith, *Op. Cit.*, p. 427.
7. *Ibid.*, p. 428.
8. *Ibid.*, p. 438.
9. *Ibid.* p. 439.
10. *Ibid.*

10. The Political Struggle of the Dispossessed (1909—1960)

Political awakening among the people of Azania

The Battle of Isandhlwana in January 1879, was the last major battle of national resistance in Azania fought against settler colonialism. By the early eighteen eighties, Africans were already realizing that they needed something more powerful than assegais against the settler's guns. They decided to opt for political struggle rather than a military campaign. Interestingly it was the Christians who first moved in this direction. A number of educated African Christians began to question the inequality of opportunities.

African Christian leaders began to agitate to break away from White churches. Rev Nehemiah Tile, an African Methodist minister broke away from the Methodist Church and formed the Tembuland National Church. In 1892 Rev Mangena Mokone followed suit and formed the Ethiopian Church in Pretoria. Many othr African church leaders also broke away. Rev James M. Dwane was one of them. He broke away in 1896 and worked both with Mokone and the Negro churches in the USA. The Black people had formed their own church in the USA in 1816 as a protest against racism within the church.

Some early Black Political Organizations

The first political organizations emerged in the 1880's. These largely grew among the Xhosa Africans of the Eastern Cape. Some of the first political organizations were: The Native Electoral Association; Imbumba Yama Afrika (Organization of United Africans). The African Political Organisation was a 'Coloured' organization. But it is significant that from the very beginning the so-called Coloureds regarded themselves as Africans, although APO membership was essentially 'Coloured' and 'Malay'. At least one member was a well known African, Solomon Platje who was to be Secretary of the South

African Native National Congress. The founder of the African Political Organization was Dr Abdul Abdurahman.

The Natal Native Congress was founded in Natal in 1900. Mark Radebe, Saul Msane, John Dube, Josiah Gumede and Martin Lutuli were foundation members. The organization's leaders were Christians who saw armed resistance as suicidal in the face of the military superiority of the white settlers backed by British imperialism.

Six years earlier in 1894 Indians, who had been brought to South Africa in 1860 by the British colonial government to work in the sugar plantations, formed their own political organization. The Natal Indian Congress was founded by Mohandas K. Ghandi who later returned to India and liberated it from British impèrialism. The indentured Indian labourers were chiefly low-caste Hindus from Bombay, Calcutta and Madras.

In 1902 another African political organization was formed in the Eastern Cape, called the South African Native Congress. In 1912 the formation of the South African Native National Congress (SANNC) was announced. Amongst its leaders were men like Dube, Rubusana, Molema, Makgatho and figures like Dr Pixley ka Seme who had founded his own newspaper *Abantu-Batho* in 1911. It was published in English and in four main African languages. In 1912, a hundred delegates attended the inaugural conference. It later became the South African National Congress. Among the delegates were nine important chiefs: Maama Seiso representing Basutoland under King Letsie II; Joshua Molema representing the paramount chief Montsioa; the Orange Free State Native Congress was represented by its President J. Mocher. Rev John Dube who was elected the ANC's first President, Solly T. Platje was elected Secretary of the African National Congress, there were seven vice-presidents, including Rubusana.[1]

The African National Congress's formation was historically significant for it gave the African people of Azania hope that one day they would reverse their military defeat through political power. In 1913 the newly formed African National Congress found itself fighting the Native Land Act which deprived Africans of large tracts of land. It was the beginning, for the ANC was to continue to fight for the welfare of the African people. They opposed the extension of pass laws to the African women in 1919; they demanded higher wages and conditions of service for the African people; and they also fought for effective parliamentary representation.

In the white parliament Africans were represented by four 'native representatives', Europeans elected by African voters in the Cape Province and Natal. There were also unrepresentative bodies such as the Native Representative Council and Advisory Boards on which a number of ANC leaders served. In 1935 a law disenfranchising the Cape Africans was introduced under the 'Hertzog's Bills'. The African's franchise was replaced by the Native Representative Council. However popular African opinion was opposed to this measure.

The All-African Convention, a political organization founded in 1935, won massive African support when it called for the rejection of all *dummy* bodies and advocated a policy of non-collaboration with the settler government. The All African Convention made this bold stand at the time when African intellectuals were vying with one another for positions on the bogus institutions for the *child race*.[2] The All African Convention argued that to continue to operate the segregated institutions for any reason whatsoever was to accept inferiority of the Black man and to involve the population in working the machinery of their own oppression.[3]

A federation of political organizations, the Non-European Unity Movement, was formed to implement the policy of non-collaboration. The All African Convention, the African National Congress and the Communist Party of South Africa were all involved. However internal divisions began to emerge. 'The younger men wanted to boycott the body entirely, whereas the older men, seeing that it was inevitable, wanted to make it work in the hope of gathering a crumb or two. The view of the elders prevailed... '[4]

Non-collaboration policy failed. The African National Congress and the Communist Party of South Africa, whose leaders were anxious to use the dummy bodies, pulled out of the Non-European Unity Movement. The All-African Convention continued to battle alone.

The Communist Party of South Africa and the ANC, having pulled out of the 'federation', filled the dummy bodies. ANC leaders took up positions on the advisory boards and the Native Representative Council, while the leaders of the Communist Party of South Africa were woeing the African vote in attempts to secure positions as the 'Native Representatives' in the white parliament. Leading South African white 'communists' like Sam Khan and Sydney Bunting were elected as 'native representatives.'

Commenting on the Native Representative Council, Chief Albert Luthuli said:

I had no connection with this Council in its early years, save, in my capacity as chief. However, when the death of Dr Dube brought about a by-election, I was voted into his place. I was interested, though not at all surprised, as I went about among the people before the election, to notice how deeply disillusioned they were by this time with the Council.

'What is the use,' they asked me, 'of your going to the NRC in Pretoria? They do nothing but talk. Where has this Council got us?'

It was only true. For years now they had talked. Nobody listened. I was disillusioned myself, and could only reply. There are people beyond South Africa who sometimes hear what we say. All we can do is to shout to the world. All I can do is to help us shout louder.[5]

Of the Native Representative Council the historian Eric A. Walker says: 'In 1937 the newly created Native Representative Council met for the first time, all good men, among the best of them being the Rev John Dube and Selope Thema, a leader of the African National Congress and editor of the *Bantu World* started by two Europeans... '[6]

But in reality 'good' leaders achieved nothing for the African people through the Native Representative Council. For instance, in 1939 members of the Native Representative Council suddenly promised the Smuts government that they would not press the claims of the African people too hard until the War was over. The African leaders probably believed that this gesture of good will would secure a better deal for the African people. Of course, the African masses were annoyed by this kind of compromise. 'In India', an African writer commented, 'Ghandi was being jailed for insisting on a clear definition of British war aims for his country. Here were representatives of an oppressed people deciding to give a new lease on life to race injustice in a war fought precisely against race humiliation.'[7]

In the late thirties and early forties the Non-Europeans in general were the most ill-organized group in South Africa argued Walker. 'Now however', he added:

the recently anti-European Youth Movement (referring to the ANC Youth League, which represented the Africanist school of thought) had galvanised the long quiescent African National Congress into such a vigorous life that Dr Alfred Xuma, the president of that Congress, could arouse enthusiasm among its members when he told them with truth that Dingaan, the villain of the Voortrekker Monument dedication, had, with all his faults, been a defender of African freedom and bade them stand firm like him in their own struggle for liberty...[8]

What was this Youth Movement? How was it anti-European

The growing restlessness of the African youth 'at lack of action led to the establishment in 1944 of the Youth League which worked within the ANC, but demanded positive measures to publicise African opposition to discrimination.'[9] The Youth League was therefore, a pressure group inside the African National Congress but which had its own basic policy, namely the overthrow of foreign domination and foreign leadership and the implementation of the fundamental right of the African people to self-determination.

One writer observed:

Quite early in history, the League had committed itself to the policy of going on the offensive in its bid to alter the pace of movement toward freedom. In pursuing this line, it had administered a fatal blow to the NRC (Native Representative Council) when it forced Professor Matthews and Dr Moroka to resign from the Council. It broke Champion's grip on the ANC in Natal and threw Dr Xuma out of office by paving the way for Albert Luthuli, whom the Natal Leaguers were steadily pushing to the fore as expressing the mood of the ANC. And when the League felt it had cleaned the Congress house sufficiently, it turned to direct action against race oppression.[10]

'The militancy urged by the ANC Youth League was finally adopted in 1949 as the programme of the Congress as a whole.'[11] The extent to which the Youth League had galvanized the African National Congress was evident in the successful 1952 Defiance Campaign of Unjust Laws. This was passive resistance in the style of Mahatma Ghandi's philosophy of non-violence. Thousands of Africans took part and several defiers were arrested, convicted and sentenced to gaol. But others went on defiantly. The Malan apartheid settler Government which had been returned to power in 1948 became increasingly alarmed by the campaign and took stiffer measures to crush it. The Boer Government declared the defiance of whiteman's laws, a serious crime punishable by flogging and extended imprisonment. The 1953 Criminal Laws Amendment

Act was enacted to deal with this 'serious crime'.

In the face of this stiff legislation, the African National Congress called off the campaign. As the defiance campaign collapsed the ANC leadership pushed for a 'multi-racial' policy to replace the programme of action and nation building advocated by the Youth League.

A Congress Alliance was formed to implement this 'multi-racial' policy. This alliance was made up of the Congress of Democrats (Europeans who were mainly former members of the Communist Party of South Africa which had dissolved itself in 1950): the Coloured People's Organization and the South African Congress of Trade Unions (SACTU); the merchant class South African Indian Congress and the African National Congress. The Alliance was co-ordinated by the National Consultative Committee which acted as a policy-making body.

Jordan K. Ngubane, an African journalist and politician who had with other members of the Youth League of the ANC fought to replace Dr. Moroka with Chief Luthuli as president of the ANC commented on the inner working of the 'multi-racial' alliance:

> On this body (National Consultative Committee), the ANC, as the largest organization in the movement and the one representing the biggest section of the nation, had as many votes as the COD, which was supported by no more than 500 people in the white community.[12]

Although in the Coloured elections for the Assembly the Coloured People's Organization had been unable to elect its candidate, it still had as many votes as Luthuli's ANC in the consultative committee. Through the 'multi-racial' Congress Alliance the ANC had been reduced to a minority organization status:

> The Youth League critics who had feared that collaboration with the other groups would lead to the humiliation of the African, pointed out that their fears had been vindicated. Multi-racialism in practice meant that the *minority* groups could gang up in the policy making body against the majority and place themselves in the position to dictate policy.[13]

When Chief Luthuli was banned and confined to his farm at Groutville, it became evident that the ANC was not its own master. Chief Luthuli had only a tenuous control of his organization. He attempted to transfer the headquarters from Johannesburg to Durban, but failed. In 1955 Dr Wilson Conco, Chief Luthuli's deputy in the ANC, chaired a meeting at Kliptown, Johannesburg at which the 'Freedom Charter' was produced. Dr Conco is said to have seen this document for the first time at Kliptown. Confirming this, a writer says that Dr Conco:

> on his return (to Durban to report to Chief Luthuli) said he had seen the document for the first time at the conference. And Luthuli himself had not known who had drafted the charter. The co-ordinating committee of the alliance was, as a matter of fact, not the real originator of policy.[14]

The white reformist Communist Party of South Africa had done all the planning.

The lack of control the leadership exerted over the ANC was often embarrassing and dangerous. Jordan K. Ngubane, once a staunch ANC member writes:

> One case will illustrate this contention. When the government threatened to eject the Africans from Sophiatown near Johannesburg, the ANC promised to lead the resistance. Luthuli, assured that the will to oppose government plans was irresistible, committed himself to the public statement, as a result of the advice he had received, that Sophiatown would be a Waterloo either for the ANC or for the government. By this he meant that the ANC would accept challenge and resist removals because the people were behind it. When the day of removals came, the subtenants dumped their goods and jumped into the police and army lorries, singing. Manilal Ghandi often used to say that he did not see any sign of the ANC resistance when the police showed up. In 1955 he had travelled especially to Johannesburg to see Luthuli's followers disgrace apartheid.[15]

Ngubane adds:

> This was not just a piece of bungling. The with-holding of vital information from Luthuli was part of the plan to destroy, whenever necessary, any African leader who was not completely under the control of the Communists (the white minority reformist 'Communist' Party of South Africa). African members of SACTU were encouraged to join the ANC and vice versa; Moses Mabhida was the Communist sponsored chief of the SACTU, and Luthuli led the ANC. Under this arrangement, the African members were deliberately given a dual

leadership as a precaution against Luthuli's defecting one day. If he were to do that, Mabhida would assert himself as SACTU leader against Luthuli. Since Mabhida was always with the workers, he stood a better chance of pulling a very substantial section of them in any showdown with Luthuli. And in any crisis not involving Luthuli, he could easily be upheld as the leader of the Africans.[16]

The Youth League unhappy that the 1949 programme of action had been shelved or surrendered to the white Communist Party of South Africa leadership, grew more restless. By 1956 the Youth League was already calling itself the 'Africanists' and founded their own publication *The Africanist*. The Africanists advocated a policy of militant action against the racist minority government. Finally, on the 2 November 1958, the Africanists left the African National Congress; the Pan Africanist Congress was founded on the 6 of April 1959.

Writing about the break, a European journalist observed:

> Once again the African nationalist movement was split between two rival organizations, but this time, in contrast to the earlier split between the ANC and AAC, the differences were not only over tactics but also over allies. Under Luthuli's leadership, the ANC had remained loyal to the Congress alliance with its white, Asian and Coloured components, in particular because this association demonstrated Luthuli's desire for a multi-racial South Africa within which people would be free to associate without regard for race or colour. To Sobukwe and the PAC, in contrast, the basis of any reconstituted society in South Africa had to be African since, they argued, it is the Africans who are indigenous to the country, form the majority of its population and provide most of its labour.
>
> The ANC and PAC also differed more than the ANC and AAC (African National Congress and All African Convention) in the constituencies to which they made their appeal. The earlier African nationalist movements concentrated on the urban literate, used English as the medium of communication, and thought in terms of change within the existing structure. Their approach was more comparable therefore, to that of American Negroes in their attempts to improve their conditions in the United States than to that of African nationalists in West Africa or East Africa with their drive for African majority

control and independence.

Many of the Pan Africanists are highly educated, Sobukwe was a lecturer at the University of Witwatersrand from 1953 until 1960, but they have made a deliberate and quite attempt to communicate their own aspirations to African migratory workers in their own native languages and through examples and idioms that the workers understand in terms of their own experiences.[17]

The PAC challenged the contemporary view that South Africa was not a colony but an 'independent' state, put forward by some of the African leaders and the white South African Communist Party.

Reporting on the historic All Africa Conference called by Dr Kwame Nkrumah in Accra in 1958, Dr Ezekiel Mphahlele an ANC delegate to the conference said,

> Dr Kiano (of Kenya) comes up. He is uncompromising and says, concepts of multi-racial society, apartheid and Batustans are traps laid by the white man. Makes me realize all the more how difficult it is to tell the colonial African, who thinks of his problem in the simplest terms of Black versus White, about our fight in South Africa to set up a multi-racial community.

Like all his colleagues, Dr Mphahlele had failed to appreciate the fact that the African people in apartheid South Africa were dispossessed in exactly the same way as the people of Kenya had been. Dr Mphahlele had also been wrong in thinking that Dr Kiano was a colonial African seeing his problem in terms of 'black versus white'. The fight was between the oppressor and the oppressed; the robber and the robbed; the dispossessor and the dispossessed. It was a struggle to establish majority rule which is democracy and destroy the minority rule of the settlers which is the negation of democracy.

Commenting on the new direction introduced by the Pan Africanist Congress, Jordan K. Ngubane said:

> Up to that time, African political organizations had not taken a clear stand on immediate participation. They had contented themselves merely with demanding equal rights for all. The PAC did not stop at demanding participation but enunciated an ideal of society it wanted to build. In this, the PAC went further than any other political group, for it was out to build an Africanist, socialist and non-racial nation.[18]

From the very beginning, the Pan Africanist Congress rejected the myth that South Africa was 'independent'. In his speech at the inaugural conference of the PAC held in Orlando Community Hall, Johannesburg on the 6 April 1959 (a date which deliberately coincided with the arrival of the first settlers in Azania on the 6 April 1652), President Mangaliso Robert Sobukwe said:

> The Europeans are a foreign group which has exclusive control of political, economic, social and military power. It is the dominant group. It is the exploiting group, responsible for the pernicious doctrine of White supremacy which has resulted in the humiliation and degradation of the indigenous African people. It is this group which has dispossessed the African people of their land and with arrogant conceit has set itself up as the 'guardian', the 'trustees,' of the Africans. It is this group which conceives of the African people as a child nation, composed of boys and girls, ranging in age from 120 years to one day. It is this group which after 300 years can still state with brazen effrontery that the Native, the Bantu, the Kaffir is still backward and savage etc. But they still want to remain 'guardians', 'trustees', and what have you, of the African people. In short, it is this group which has mismanaged affairs in South Africa. It is from this group that the most rabid race baiters and agitators come. It is members of this group who, whenever they meet in their Parliament, say things which agitate the ears of millions of peace-loving Africans. This is the group which turns out thousands of experts on that new South African science—the Native mind.

The PAC leader concluded by saying,

> I wish to state that the Africanists do not at all subscribe to the fashionable doctrine of exceptionalism. Our contention is that South Africa is an integral part of the invisible whole that is Africa. She cannot solve her problems in isolation from and with utter disregard of the rest of the continent.
>
> Against multi-racialism we have this objection, that the history of South Africa has fostered group prejudices and antagonisms, and if we have to maintain the same group exclusiveness, parading under the term multi-racialism, we shall be transporting to the new Africa these antagonisms and

conflicts. Further, multi-racialism is in fact a pandering to
European bigotry and arrogance. It is a method of safeguarding
white interests irrespective of population figures. In that sense
it is a complete negation of democracy. To us the term 'multi-
racialism' implies that there are such basic insuperable differences between the various national groups here that the best
course is to keep them permanently distinctive in a kind of
democratic apartheid. That to us is racialism multiplied, which
probably is what the term truly connotes.

We aim, politically, at government of the Africans by the
Africans, for the Africans, with everybody who owes his only
loyalty to Africa and who is prepared to accept the democratic
rule of an African majority being regarded as an African. We
guarantee no minority rights, because we think in terms of individuals, not groups.

Economically, we aim at the rapid extension of industrial
development in order to alleviate pressure on the land which is
what progress means in terms of modern society. We stand
committed to a policy of guaranteeing the most equitable
distribution of wealth.

Socially, we aim at the full development of the human personality and a ruthless and outlawing of all forms of or
manifestations of racial myth. To sum it up we stand for an
Africanist Socialist Democracy... *Izwe Lethu* (The country is
Ours!)[19]

Sobukwe's speech clearly reflected the new mood of the country's
youth and the African masses. The Pan Africanist Congress adopted two
slogans: 'Africa for Africans, Africans for humanity and humanity for
God' and 'Izwe Lethu' (the country is ours!). Their motto was 'Service,
Sacrifice and Suffering.' The new militant organization emerged with
its own form of national salute, freedom songs, flag and so on. Its leaders
proclaimed an unfolding programme. First they would stage a status campaign and launch a positive action campaign against the hated pass laws.

The Pan Africanist Congress's formation was greeted by the settler
press describing the new organisation as 'extremist and racialist and planning to drive the white man to the sea.' They blamed this 'extremism'
on the South African government's refusal to listen to the moderate
African National Congress. The ANC itself through its Secretary-General
Duma Nokwe described PAC and its policies as 'Black intransigence

equally demented.' Ronald Segal, a European settler who later joined the ANC charged the PAC with being a 'manifestation of the black racialism that had developed in response to the white racialism of apartheid.'

The 'Communist' Party of South Africa for its part led a vicious campagin of abuse against the PAC and its policies, and personally attacked its leaders. Potlako K. Leballo was a favourite target for invectiveness. As one journalist puts it:

Communist journalists projected an image of him in which he was represented as a hard, insensitive, dull-witted race hater... and a mob-rousing mountbank. The rest of the white press took the cue: Leballo became South Africa's bogeyman Number One.

The individual behind the bogeyman, however, was a fierce hater of race oppression. He had felt its reality in his own life. When World War II broke out, he had suffered so much from it that he left school, volunteered for service, and fought courageously by the side of white men to destroy Nazi racialism. The man who had inspired Potlako to risk his life in this fight was a white man, none other than Hofmeyer, a Cabinet Minister in the Smuts Government. Hofmeyer had gone on a recruiting tour to Lovedale College to explain to the African students the issues at stake in the war.[20]

The PAC leaders were unpreturbed by the attacks on themselves and their organization. For them the struggle for South Africa was of primary importance for it was 'part of the greater struggle throughout the continent for the restoration to the African people of the effective control of their land.'[21]

The PAC launched the status campaign. Its purpose was clearly outlined at a meeting by Mangaliso Sobukwe when he said:

Now, for over three hundred years, the white foreign ruling minority has used its power to inculcate in the African a feeling of inferiority. This group has educated the African to accept the *status quo* of White supremacy and Black inferiority as normal.

It is our task to exorcise this slave mentality, and to impart to the African masses that sense of self-reliance which will make them choose 'to starve in freedom rather than have plenty in bondage', the self-reliance that will make them prefer self-government to the good government (of whites) preferred by the ANC leader (a reference to Chief Luthuli's claim that he would not mind being ruled by European settlers provided their government was just).

It must be clearly understood that we are not begging the foreign minorities to treat our people courteously. We are calling on our people to assert their personality. We are reminding our people that they are men and women with children of their own and homes of their own, and that just as much as they resent being called *kwedini* or *umfana* or *moshemane* by us—which is what 'boy' means—they must equally resent such terms of address by the foreigner. We are reminding our people that acceptance of any indignity, any insult, any humiliation, is acceptance of inferiority. They must first think of themselves as men and women before they can demand to be treated as such.

Although, the ANC proclaimed the defiance campaign in 1952, it was actually initiated in the 1949 as part of the Programme of Action. As Ernest Harsh points out in his book *South Africa: White Rule, Black Revolt*:

Most significantly, the Youth League's Programme of Action, initially presented the year before, was adopted as official ANC policy, signaling a significant shift in the organisation's political orientation. It went beyond the ANC's earlier timid calls for abolition of legal discrimination and recognition of equality of opportunity. It now demanded no less than 'freedom from White domination and the attainment of political independence'. This implies the rejection of the conception of segregation, apartheid, trusteeship, or White leadership which are all in one way or another motivated by the ideas of White domination or domination of Whites over the Blacks. Like all other people the African people claim the right of self-determination. This was to be achieved under the banner of African Nationalism.[22]

As a result of the adoption of the defiance campaign, ANC membership increased from 7,000 to 100,000. 'For the first time,' observed Ernest Harsh, 'in its history, the ANC had a real mass base.'

In 1955 the ANC officially adopted the 'Freedom' Charter and abandoned the fight for self-determination and national sovereignty in Azania.

The ANC's de-emphasizing of the national character of the

struggle was accompanied by greater overtures to white 'opposition' circles. This approach involved the erroneous conception that it was the National Party alone that was primarily responsible for segregation and other facets of national oppression, rather than the ruling class as a whole.[23]

Even the (English) United Party which was then the official 'opposition' in South Africa, was invited to the Kliptown Indaba where the Kliptown Charter was adopted.

Ernest Harsh observes that the so-called Communist Party of South Africa which had dissolved itself in 1950 after the threat of the Suppression of the Communist Act, 'had re-organized underground about two years later as the South African Communist Party (SACP). Because of its hostility to militant African nationalism and its policy of seeking blocs with white 'democratic' bourgeois forces, it bore a certain amount of responsibility for this mutation in the ANC policies.[24]

References:
1. H.J. and R.E. Simmons, *Class and Colour in South Africa 1850—1950*, p. 134.
2. *The Revolutionary Road for South Africa*, by the Unity Movement of South Africa, p. 17.
3. Jordan K. Ngubane, *An African Explains Apartheid*, p. 91.
4. Albert Luthuli, *Let My People Go*, p. 102.
5. *Ibid.*, p.103.
6. Eric A. Walker, *Op. Cit.*, p. 647.
7. Jordan K. Ngubane, *Op. Cit.*, p. 96.
8. Eric A. Walker, *Op. Cit.*, p. 793.
9. John A. Davis and James K. Baker (ed.), *Southern Africa in Transition*, p. 9.
10. Jordan K. Ngubane, *Op. Cit.*, p. 98.
11. John A. Davis and James K. Baker, *Op. Cit.*, p. 9.
12. Jordan K. Ngubane, *Op. Cit.*, p. 100.
13. *Ibid.*, p. 100-101.
14. *Ibid.*, p. 164.
15. *Ibid.*, p. 165.
16. Jordan K. Ngubane, *An African Explains Apartheid*, p. 165.
17. John A. Davis and James K. Baker, *Op. Cit.*, p. 11-12.
18. Jordan K. Ngubane, *Op. Cit.*, p. 102.
19. *The Basic Documents of the Pan Africanist Congress of South Africa*, p. 15-16.

20. Jordan K. Ngubane, *Op. Cit.*, p. 101-102.
21. *The Basic Documents of the Pan Africanist Congress of South Africa*, p. 15-16.
22. Ernest Harsch, *SOUTH AFRICA White Rule Black Revolt*, p. 125.
23. *Ibid.*, p. 233.
24. *Ibid.*

11. Sharpeville Closed the Old Chapter

After the success of the status campaign the PAC decided it was time to launch the positive action campaign against the pass laws. Mangaliso Sobukwe and other PAC leaders toured the country from Johannesburg to Capetown, explaining that their Party was ready to launch the campaign. The African people welcomed the news. The leaders told their members and supporters to stock food and that on a date to be announced each member or supporter of the Pan Africanist Congress would have to leave his pass at home and go to the police station and ask the police to arrest him.

Opposition to the campaign came not only from the White press, but also from the ANC leadership. When Sobukwe, through the PAC National Secretary, invited the African National Congress to join hands in the campaign. The ANC rejected it through their Secretary-General, Duma Nokwe, who published his reply in the *Sunday Times* in Johannesburg on the 20 March 1960. It read: 'It is treacherous to the liberation movement to embark on a campaign which has not been prepared and which has no reasonable prospects of success.' However, the Pan Africanist Congress had already announced the date for the planned campaign against the passes, and on the 21 March, the campaign was launched.

In his book, *The Anatomy of Apartheid*, E.S. Sachs says, 'At numbers of police stations in widely scattered areas the demonstrations went off according to plan. Sobukwe and a number of his companions, for example, presented themselves without passes at the Orlando police station in Johannesburg, and were arrested.'[1] The campaign gained enthusiastic support in many parts of the country. At Sharpeville and at Langa crowds of 20,000 and 30,000 respectively joined. 'Black Monday' 21 March 1960, 83 people were killed and 365 wounded. Several of the PAC leaders were arrested, including Mangaliso Sobukwe, Potlako Leballo, Zephania Mothopeng, Selby Ngendane, Philip Kgosana, George Zwide Siwisa, Josiah Madzunya, and Mlamli Makwetu.

At Sharpeville, Langa in Capetown, at Vanderbijl Park and elsewhere, massacres took place. The shootings angered Africans and the world alike. Even those of the ANC who had refused to take part in the pass campaign were embroiled.

On 24 March in a bid to control the situation, the Government banned meetings in 265 magisterial districts of South Africa. On the 28 March the Unlawful Organization Bill was introduced, empowering the Governor-General to ban the Pan Africanist Congress; the African National Congress was also banned, after 48 years of existence. On 30 March, the army was mobilized. On the same day 1,569 people from the South African Indian Congress, the Liberal Party, the Congress of Democrats, the Pan Africanist Congress and the African National Congress were arrested under the newly declared State of Emergency. On 22 April the Minister of Justice, Erasmus confirmed the arrests: 94 whites, 24 coloureds and 1,451 Bantu.

Protests continued to occur. On 30 March an estimated 60,000 crowd of Africans from Langa and Nyanga in Capetown gathered at the Caledon Square police station demanding their leaders release. In Stellenbosch, Africans marched from Kaya Mandi township to take part in the campaign but the armed police baton charged angrily and dispersed them. As the police left, government offices were set on fire; a church, clinic and some homes belonging to suspected informers were also burnt. African youths stoned passing Europeans cars. The skiet commando had to be rushed to the area to patrol it day and night.

On 28 March, in both Worcester and Zwelitsha, buildings were set alight: six churches, one school and a civic centre were destroyed at the value of £30,000. On 31 March over 3,000 Africans marched to the Mayville police station to be arrested for refusing to carry their passes. Earlier about 900 Africans had marched to the Magistrate Court and burned their passes. At Muizenburg they burnt a school; at Cato Manor in Durban 10,000 people marched to the pass office but were turned away by a detachment of an armed baton charge.

On the 4 May, Sobukwe, Mothopeng, Leballo, Ngendane and others were convicted and sentenced to prison from between 18 months to 3 years. 'The magistrate took 135 minutes to deliver his judgement. The evidence showed that the PAC has its ultimate object the overthrow of what was called white supremacy. The abolition of pass laws was the first step to that goal.'[2] When sentencing the PAC leaders the magistrates said, 'Not only was it your object to fill the gaols, but you intended to paralyse trade, industry and the economy of the country, in order to force the Government to change laws.' But Sobukwe's speech on behalf of his colleagues inspired Azanians especially when he said:

> Your worship, it will remembered that when this case began we refused to plead, because we felt no moral obligation whatsoever to obey laws which are made exclusively by a white minority... But I would like to quote what was said by somebody before—that an unjust law cannot be justly applied.
>
> We believe in one race only—the human race to which we all belong. The history of that race is a long struggle against all restrictions, physical, mental and spiritual.
>
> We would have betrayed the human race if we had not done our share. We are glad to have made our contribution.
>
> We stand for equal rights for *all individuals*. But the whites have to accept allegiance to Africa first; once a truly non-racial democracy exists in South Africa, all individuals, whatever their colour or race, will be accepted as Africans.
>
> As individuals we do not count; we are but the tools of history, which will always find new tools. We are not afraid of the consequences of our action and it is not our intention to plead for mercy. Thank you, Your Worship.'

At the beginning of the trial the PAC leader and his colleagues had said, 'The law under which we are charged is a law made exclusively by the white man, and the officers administering the law are white men. We do not see how justice can be done in these circumstances.'

The PAC leaders were jailed and both the PAC and ANC banned. The 'Sharpeville' campaign had not achieved the abolition of passes nor the ultimate overthrow of the government. But Sharpeville shook the whole country and changed its political climate.

Sharpeville worried businessmen enormously. The Chamber of Commerce and Industries handed a memorandum to the Government which said:

> The immediate cost has been loss of life, loss of production, general unrest, and diversion of part of our manpower to military service. Far more serious is the loss of confidence among investors in South Africa abroad, resulting in the withdrawal of capital and cancellation of business projects that were under favourable consideration; the potential loss of people

through emigration and reduced immigration, and the damage that the economy sustains as a result of mounting international disapproval of the policies being followed in South Africa, which are widely believed to have caused the present crisis.

Further damage to the country's economy was witnessed when for the first quarter of 1960 alone capitalization value of shares quoted on the stock exchange dropped by £600,000,000. In one day alone on March 30th, the total market capitalisation value was slashed down by £70,000,000.

The South African Bank Reserves sank to their lowest level ever. This damaged economy which nearly brought about an African majority rule in Azania was saved by the United States of America. America provided financial aid to the tune of £100,000,000. American banks such as Chase Manhattan, First National City Bank of New York, Irving Trust Company, Morgan Guaranty Trust, Bank of America, Manufacturers Hanover Trust, Continental Illinois National Bank, First National Bank of Chicago and Bankers Trust Company ignored the blood of the Azanians killed in Sharpeville, Langa and other places, and revived the devastated economy of settler South Africa.

Assassination of Settler Prime Minister Verwoerd

The unprecedented loss of money and damage to the South African economy caused great anxiety among the businessmen and led to an attempted assassination of the Prime Minister, Dr Hendrick Verwoerd.
As one journalist put it,

The shooting in an attempted assassination of Dr Verwoerd... was the most propitious and accurate weather signal for the era ushered in by Sharpeville. The incident took place at the height of the 1960 crisis on 9 April, when Dr Verwoerd was addressing a big crowd at the opening of the Union Exposition at the show-ground in Johannesburg.

Though unplanned, the incident was politically motivated, and was inspired by the campaign. Some have attempted to belittle the political significance of the shot fired by David Pratt, who was later adjudged by a court to be of unsound mind.

On his own account, David Pratt, a wealthy farmer, was driven to desperation by the Prime Minister's shiftlessness in his granite apartheid attitude in the show-ground speech which took no notice of the tremendous harm done to the country's economy by the policies which had led to the Sharpeville crisis.

As business man at a trade fair, Pratt was disturbed, as he said, by the Prime Minister's indifference to what was happening in the country. He may have had certain delusions, as it has been alleged, but it is a fact that the whole business world of South Africa was disturbed by these events...

The South African Government found the situation so difficult to control that on the 25 March they suspended the pass law for 17 days and instructed the police not to arrest any African found without one. It was a victory for the PAC. Everywhere people were speaking about the 'PAC chaps'. In fact, on the following day Chief Luthuli was advised by the White liberals to burn his own pass.

Reporting on the effect the Sharpeville campaign had on the Government, Lewis Nkosi, then a reputable journalist who generally supported the more moderate ANC, wrote,

...a tall, distinguished-looking African prisoner, a university instructor and a political leader, who, at the age of 36, had a rare distinction of having scared Dr Verwoerd's government out of its wits.' As anybody knows by now, the South African Government does not scare easily.

In March 1960 Robert Sobukwe, President of the banned Pan Africanist Congress, helped to orchestrate a crisis that panicked the South African Government and nearly brought about the kind of political anarchy which all too often makes possible the transference of power overnight.[3]

Paul Sauer, acting Prime Minister in Dr Verwoerd's absence, spoke at Humansdorp in the Cape Province 15 days after PAC leaders had been sentenced. Sauer said:

The old book of South African history was closed a month ago, and, for the immediate future, South Africa will reconsider in earnest and honestly her whole approach to the Native question. We must create a new spirit which must restore overseas faith—both white and non-white in South Africa... We must alter the conception of baaskap (white boss mentality) in areas which will be made available by the government to the Bantu—there should be absolutely no reference to baaskap. .

The apartheid settlers found these sentiments intolerable, accused Sauer of having gone too far.

The Minister of Justice, Francois Erasmus, told Parliament in a quivering voice: 'Their (PAC) aim is to bring to its knees *any* White Government in South Africa which stands for White supremacy and White leadership. They do not want peace and order; what they want is not a £1 a day for all the Bantu in South Africa. *What they want is our country!*'*

On the 8 April 1960 legislation was hurried through the racist Parliament banning the Pan Africanist Congress. The ANC was also banned although white liberals argued that only the Pan Africanist Congress should be banned.

The author of *Martyrs and Fanatics: South Africa and the Human Destiny*, Peter Dreyer writes, 'Len Lee-Warden, MP the CODite Natives' Representative for the Cape Western, now committed the signal indecency of pleading in Parliament that the government *ban only the PAC*.[4] Lee-Warden, associated with the Communist Party of South Africa, put his case against the banning of the ANC:

> ...if ever there was a need, it exists today for the Government to realize that it has in the ANC a friend and not an enemy, because these organizations that we are asked to ban are so diametrically opposed that the Government should seize the opportunity of appealing to the ANC to assist it to restore peace and order in South Africa.

Sharpeville had clearly transformed the political thinking of the African people. Commenting on the political thinking after Sharpeville, Jordan K. Ngubane says,

> One very important result of this was that the white authority, as its habit, shot the Africans at Sharpeville in 1960 to assert white initiatives, the gulf between the two moods was bridged... Criticisim of peaceful methods was bolder, for increasing numbers of people argued that mass non-violence was an incitement to state violence... In short a change was taking place in the thinking of the African.

---

* The ANC and the South African Trade Union had been demanding a £1 a day for years.

Another cruel dilemma was emerging. It was becoming clear that the day was not far off when the choice before South Africa would be between the guerrilla with a grenade or gun in his hand and the saboteur with a box of matches in his pocket. The 'extremist' would be the guerrilla; the 'moderate' the saboteur, so violent and extreme were the contradictions in the race crisis.[5]

Ngubane was soon proved correct. In 1961 Nelson Mandela of the traditionally moderate ANC announced the formation of *Umkhonto Wesizwe*—sabotage group. When he was arrested in 1962 he echoed Sobukwe's words of May 1960. Mandela told the court that he was

neither legally nor morally bound to obey laws made by a Parliament in which I have no representation. In a political trial such as this one, which involves a clash of the aspirations of the African people and those of the whites, the country's courts, as presently constituted, cannot be impartial and fair... It is fit and proper to raise the question sharply, what is this rigid colour bar in the administration of justice? Why is that in this court-room I face a white magistrate, confronted by a white prosecutor, and escorted into the dock by a white orderly? Can anyone honestly and seriously suggest that in this type of atmosphere the scales of justice are evenly balanced?

Sharpeville was not the first massacre of Africans, between 1919 and 1960 twenty one known cases occurred. In 1920 members of a religious sect under Enock Mgijima 130 people were killed. In 1946 striking miners in Johannesburg were killed. In Witzshoek, Sekhukhuniland, Mbizana in Pondoland and elsewhere there have been similar massacres of the Black people. But Sharpeville was unique in that it was a country-wide uprising with its ultimate goal the seizure of political power.

It is not surprising that even the international community recognized the nature of the incident. On the 2 December 1968, the General Assembly of the United Nations adopted the Resolution 2396 (XXIII): that the 21 March each year be commemorated as the International Day for the Elimination of Racial Discrimination.

On 23 March 1970, the Tanzanian newspaper *The Nationalist* editorial said:

There is no gain saying the fact that when the annals of the liberation of Southern Africa and of Azania in particular, come to be written, Sharpeville will assume the prominence of a historical watershed. For the incident demonstrated the courage of Azanians in pursuit of their rights; it demonstrated the lengths to which they were prepared to go in sacrifice. But even more importantly it showed the limits of peaceful negotiation. Ultimately what the massacre of Sharpeville demonstrated was the utter viciousness of the South African fascists, and the need for new forms of struggle against the regime if the Azanian liberation was to be attained.

Commenting on the significance of the Sharpeville Uprising, Peter N. Raboroko, a prominent Azanian historian wrote that the effects of the positive action campaign are today legendary:

The 1960 positive action campaign marked the first major confrontation between the antagonistic forces of African nationalism led by the Pan Africanist Congress and the forces of apartheid colonialism led by the settler regime on the South African battle-field. In this confrontation the Pan Africanist Congress and the African people scored signal victory over the forces of oppression...

The campaign generated an unprecedented mood of insurrection which has remained a permanent feature of the South African situation. The specific mention of this campaign as the first step towards the overthrow of White domination and attainment of freedom and independence was unprecedented in the annals of the South African liberation...[6]

Of Sharpeville, Mangaliso Robert Sobukwe was forced to say:

we overcame the fear of the consequences of the disobeying colonial laws... It became respectable to go to jail and emerge as what Kwame Nkrumah called 'Prison Graduates'. We stripped the white man of that weapon against us.

The white man now, in Soweto, had to fall back on his ultimate weapon, the gun. Soweto has been a lesson in overcoming the fear of the gun. And now that he relies on the gun and we too can get the gun, confrontation is inevitable...

References:
1. E.S. Sachs, *The Anatomy of Apartheid*, p. 307.
2. *Ibid.*, p. 327.
3. *Africa Report*, April 1962.
4. Peter Dreyer, *Martyrs and Fanatics: South Africa and the Human Destiny*, p. 174-175.
5. Jordan K. Ngubane, *Op. Cit.*, p.136-137.
6. David Dube, *The Significance of Sharpeville*, p. 6.

12. POQO the Menace of Apartheid South Africa

After Sharpeville Africans could no longer hold political meetings or publicly discuss their national affairs. But it soon became clear that their aspirations could not be banned. New freedom songs were sung. One of these was:

> Ngalonyaka ka 1960 sahambela kwa Ntsasana
> Amapasi sawashiya nabafazi emakhaya
> Impendulo zimbumbulu, impendulo yakukufa
> Sinombuzo Velevutha, sinombuzo weVostere
> Elogazi lamaAfrika siyabuza layaphi na?
> Sadutyulwa eSharpeville sadutyulwa nakwaLanga.

(That is to say in 1960 we went to the police stations. We left our passes with our women at home. The settler police answer to our action was bullets. They killed us. We have a question to put to you Verwoerd and Vorster. We were shot at Sharpeville and Langa. What happened to the blood of those African people?).

News of the PAC was scarce, except in 1961 during a stay home organized by the ANC which was given wide publicity by the English press. The stay home was a protest against South Africa becoming a republic outside the Commonwealth, from 31 May 1961 on. Through their underground channels PAC leaders told the African people not to engage themselves in futile demonstrations. They pointed out that the 1910 Union of South Africa had been a union of oppression and suppression, and the fact that South Africa was then becoming a Republic made no difference. Africans had been as oppressed under the British monarchy and the governor-general. They said that in effect the opposition to South Africa becoming a republic had come from the English section of the ruling settler population. This section was unscrupulously using the African people in an issue that had nothing to do with their own aspirations.

Information filtering from the underground indicated that the

African people were organizing secretly themselves. The banning of the political organizations had not stopped their legitimate national aspirations. PAC cells were being organized. Their names were designed to divert the attention of the secret police. Some cells posed as football clubs, others as dance or music schools. Some were simply known as *Into ayibizwa* (the thing whose name is never revealed and mentioned) while others simply called themselves POQO. The police could not prosecute members of these 'organizations' for furthering the aims of PAC.

'POQO' soon became the most popular name. More so, because these were the most militant members of the military wing of the PAC which was armed with pangas, axes, home-made bombs and a few stolen pistols and guns. The name 'POQO' was also popular because it meant 'genuine' or 'pure' African patriots. At the beginning of 1962 newspapers began to speak of POQO.

Clashes with the police and army or with supporters of pro-apartheid government chiefs became common. Some of these clashes took place at Ntlonze and Queenstown. But the most serious was on 22 November 1962, the Paarl uprising, which resulted in a fierce attack on the police station, probably in an attempt to capture arms. In the ensuing struggle, two European policemen were killed and several wounded.

The settler government and its supporters was alarmed and immediately appointed a Commission of Enquiry into the country's armed uprisings. Mr Justice Synman, a judge of the Witwatersrand Supreme Court conducted the enquiries. The information he received revealed a very explosive situation which might immediately erupt, unless the government took stern action. Justice Snyman quickly prepared and submitted an interim report recommending that the government prevent the PAC from launching a nation-wide uprising which might lead to much violence and bloodshed, as PAC forces clashed with the police and the army. The Judge also revealed the PAC and POQO to be the same thing. He warned that other innocent-looking organizations might be connected with PAC and recommended a special law banning POQO be immediately introduced.

POQO was equated at this time with the Mau Mau of Kenya which had brought about Kenya's liberation. On the 4 February 1963, at Bashee Bridge five settlers were reportedly killed with home-made bombs and pangas. At first the government denied that the killings were politically motivated. But newspapers contradicted official government reports by revealing that POQO was responsible.

A number of uprisings and clashes between POQO forces and settler police continued to occur. Africans who acted as informers and spies for the settler government were being eliminated by POQO.

It soon became clear that the uprisings were being organized from the headquarters of the Pan Africanist Congress in Maseru, in the British colony of Lesotho. Britain could not allow the PAC to continue to undermine the government of South Africa for British investment in South Africa was £2000,000,000. To protect their investments the British government took an unprecedented step of openly collaborating with the South African police on 1 April 1963, in a surprise raid on the headquarters of the PAC, several documents and a list of names and addresses of members of the PAC inside South Africa were removed.

Immediately after this, the South African newspapers carried stories of a PAC plot to overthrow the government. In Maseru and in South Africa several PAC leaders, members and suspects were arrested; a total 10,000 Pan Africanist Congress members were arrested.

South Africa then hurriedly passed a special law to detain Mangaliso Sobukwe, the PAC President, who was due to be released early in May 1963. Sobukwe, was sent to Robben Island where he was detained without trial under a law specially enacted for him—the 'Sobukwe Clause'.

In a bid to crush Poqo or PAC, draconian laws permitting the detention of a person for 90 and 180 days without trial. Many people were dying in jail. The most publicized being Looksmart Ngudla, James Lentsoe, Babla Salooje and Abdullah Heron. Others like Zephania Mothopeng, one of the Pan Africanist Congress' top leaders, survived the torture and described the experience. Reporting Mothopeng's case, the *Star* in Johannesburg said:

> Mr Zephania Mothopeng is applying for leave to institute a pauper's suit against the Minister of Justice for R5000... Mr Mothopeng claims that he was hit and kicked and later made to undress. His hands were tied and a stick was placed under his knees and above his elbow. A canvas bag placed over his head, he alleges, and while in this position he was hit and kicked and told repeatedly, Speak! Speak!...
>
> The petition says that Mr Mothopeng alleges his body was 'jerking violently'... He heard a 'crackling vibrating noise' ... When he arrived back at another prison he felt weak and sick, his whole body was in pain, his fingers burned and his body was shaking. He felt as if he was 'going off his head'.[1]

Attempts to Crush Poqo

The courts which tried PAC or POQO suspects in 1963 handed out severe prison sentences. Several PAC leaders and activists received life imprisonment. Samuel Chibane, Philimon Tefu, John Nkosi, Jafta Masemola, Isaac Mthimunye and Dimake Malepe were sentenced for life. A year later, in 1964 after the 'Revonia trial', Nelson Mandela, Walter Sisulu, Govan Mbeki and two other ANC activists joined the PAC activists on Robben Island.

These prison sentences meted out to PAC members were intended to deter the Africans from furthering the aims of the Pan Africanist Congress. But they answered: 'Our country shall be free! We shall never stop fighting for it,' from the docks. As they were being taken to the cells they sang freedom songs such as: *Abantwana beAfrika bayakhala. Bakhalela izwe labo elathathwa ngamabulu* (The sons and daughters of Afrika are crying for their fatherland which was taken from them by the settlers. Leave our country alone, you settlers).

John Balthazar Vorster then Minister of Justice in Dr Verwoerds' Government worked tirelessly to crush the POQO/PAC. Each time he claimed that he had broken the back of POQO there would be more reported PAC activity. He had to admit that 'POQO keeps on showing its head.' The executive chief of the secret police confirmed this. The *Sunday Express* in Johannesburg reported him in 1968, eight years after the PAC was banned, as saying that the PAC had underground cells all over the country, and that the settlers should not be surprised if POQO/PAC kept on showing up.

The government intensified its campaign to indescribably crush the PAC in 1963. POQO political prisoners were maltreated, involving even sodomy. Lindiso Richard Galela's affidavit reveals some of the methods which were used to crush PAC militants.

> During all the period I spent in Robben Island, it was the daily practice of one Van Zyl, First Aid Attendant of the Prison Staff, to push his finger into my rectum and those of my working colleagues every evening on our return from work. This had an adverse effect on my health and I received no medical attention when I complained about this. Similarly when I injured my left ankle at work in September 1963, I received no medical treatment.
>
> I now want to comment on the life of Pan Africanist

Congress prisoners on Robben Island, and the conditions under which they lived while I was there.

The attitude of the white warders towards them is one of contempt, even vengeance and persecution, and goes beyond the purpose of imprisonment as understood the world over. There is no redress against the atrocities committed against them by the warders or other prisoners at the instigation and with the connivance of the warders...

Nelson Komane is a boy of sixteen years of age from Pretoria. He was viciously assaulted by a prisoner called Billy when he refused to take part in an immoral sodomy act... This matter was reported to Chief Warder Theron. Billy made counter charges with the result that Nelson was sentenced to sixteen days in solitary confinement, while Billy went off scot free. It is common practice for the young convicted boys of PAC to be forcibly locked into cells with hardened criminals and forced to commit sodomy. They can be heard shouting and calling in the night, and the warders ignore the calls. Anyone else who intervenes or takes the matter up with the prison authorities is severely punished...

Maqubela was made to stand upright in a deep hole which was then filled with soil up to his neck, with only the head appearing above the ground. Then a white warder urinated above his head and face...

Solomon Petla a boy of sixteen years of age was forced to commit sodomy and held down while he was being criminally assaulted through his anus. As a result his rectum protruded outwards, and for over three months he was unable to walk well. He lodged a complaint with one Lietenant Pretorius, who answered that his testicles should be pulled out. In addition to getting no redress for this atrocity, Petla received no medical treatment whatsoever, and his assailants continued their bestial acts upon him.

David Feni was shot prior to his commitment to Robben Island, and retains a bullet in his body. It is said that the doctor who treated him in hospital maintained that removal of the bullet would be fatal. Despite this, Feni had been allocated to do the most heavy manual labour... breaking stones and boring rocks with a machine...

The PAC prisoners were not broken by these brutal methods. In fact, imprisonment of many PAC activists worked to the advantage of POQO. More hardened criminals were being politicized and made to see their own hope in the overthrow of the white foreign government. These new recruits were extremely ruthless with those who gave PAC secrets to the prison warders.

On 24 April 1965, a Johannesburg daily newspaper the *Star* reported the following story:

> Six long-term African convicts, who 'tried' a fellow gang member and executed him, are to die for his murder.
>
> This week the six men had to be hustled shouting to the cells below in Pretoria Court after they had been sentenced to death for strangling Mhlokonjo Madellela in Baviaanspoort prison cell.
>
> The judge found that the men had conspired to kill Madellela because they believed him to be an informer who had given secrets of thier gang, the Pan Africanist Congress, to prison authorities...
>
> The gang adopted the cliches and slogans of the Pan Africanist Congress and had a president, prime minister and a speaker of the house.
>
> Mr Justice Hiemstra said that after Madellela had been condemned to die, the gang members sang (freedom songs) in the cell...

These prisoners had never previously belonged to PAC. The PAC message was taken into jail by the political prisoners mixing with hardened criminals. The men involved in the Pretoria case were Victor Mahlangu, Isaaka Masigo, Cylion Mabaso, Corry Tyimi, Joel Leballo and Phineas Mtotywa.

This was not an isolated incident. In Leeukop, a prison for the most hardened criminals, Petros Motswane, Hector Kuka, Jeremiah Maokosone and Aaron Fakude were sentenced to six years imprisonment for conspiracy to commit violence and for furthering the aims of the Pan Africanist Congress even in jail!

Before the Sharpeville Uprising these things were unheard of. But Paul Sauer had been right in his Humansdorp speech, 'The old book of South African history was closed a month ago, and for the immediate future, South Africa will reconsider in earnest and honestly her whole approach to the Native question.'

Indeed, it was not only the government that was concerned about the state of affairs in South Africa. The European public was also concerned. The South African Institute of Race Relations conducted a scientific survey into the strength of the political parties, and published their results:

Party	PAC	ANC	Liberal	Progressive	C.O.D.
For	57%	39%	31%	30%	18%
Against	29%	41%	47%	43%	42%
Undecided	14%	20%	22%	27%	40%

South Africa renamed AZANIA

The PAC had held a conference in 1964 at which the PAC underground cells were re-organized. But the number of regions was raised from an undisclosed number to 28, under 28 regional commanders.

Immediately after this conference South Africa was renamed AZANIA. The settler troops were mobilized when news of the new name leaked out for it was feared that the renaming of the country was a prelude to a planned uprising. It seems, however, that no uprising was planned. But many Africans felt that the renaming of South Africa was in keeping with the African revolution for it meant 'Blackman's country.' South Africa was a name associated with the forces of imperialism. The Gold Coast, Nyasaland and Northern Rhodesia had even been renamed before independence, Ghana, Malawi and Zambia respectively by the people aspiring to freedom, independence and nationhood.

Names such as Azanian Peoples Organisation, Azanian Students Organisation, Azania Students Movement, Black Consciousness Movement of Azania, Azania National Youth Union and so on demonstrate the acceptance of the name Azania. Only a few have resisted the change, influenced by the white settlers.

More plots against South Africa

In 1965 fifteen months after Vorster had claimed to have broken the back of POQO, another plot to overthrow the South African government was uncovered. It was alleged the plot was hatched by the PAC leadership in Maseru, Lesotho. The plot, it was said involved the blowing up of installations in South Africa and the kidnapping of government officials. The victims would be held as ransom for the release of Mangaliso

Sobukwe who had been imprisoned without trial on Robben Island under the 'Sobukwe Clause'. It was the British colonial government in Lesotho which uncovered the plot and reported it to the government in Pretoria. The arrest of PAC leaders such as John Nyati Pokela, Mfanasekhaya Gqobose and others followed. They were charged under the 1963 'Prevention of Violence Abroad Proclamation' Act.

Support for the PAC increased despite the persecution of British colonial Government in Lesotho and the South African Government. In March 1966 the leaders of the Coloured Peoples' Congress declared:

> That the South African Coloured Peoples' Congress is dissolved; recognises the revolutionary character of the Pan Africanist Congress, and announce our acceptance of their comradely invitation to join the PAC as Africans and equals, dedicate ourselves to the building up of the nation and wage a single struggle against the common enemy of white supremacy and its foreign backers who have made our country their looting ground.
>
> Call on the South African Coloureds and Indians numbering two and half million enslaved people to follow our example by becoming members of the dynamic Pan Africanist Congress, and for all time bury their racial tags.
>
> Signed:
>
> Barney Desai (President)
> Kenneth Jordan
> (Member of the Executive)
> Cardiff Marney (Secretary)

This was a recognition of the PAC as representing the interests of the Coloureds. The PAC had declared its attitude towards the Coloureds immediately after its inception: 'As far as Coloureds are concerned, they are a product of miscegenation between white and black people. Therefore, we regard them as Africans because they have no other home other than Africa.'

'From as far back as 1960,' T.M. Ntantala, then a PAC commander said in an interview with the writer,

> Messrs R.M. Sobukwe, P.K. Leballo, S.T. Ngendane and the late Howard Ngcobo during their tour of the Cape met John Gomas who wanted the above declaration discussed and once he was clear on this issue, he joined the PAC. From then, several

underground branches were formed and the Coloured people took their rightful place in the PAC as fellow Africans and an integral part of the dispossessed people of Azania. The most significant aspect of this matter is that this response came from the working elements of the Coloured people who had nothing to fear from completely identifying themselves with the African masses.

PAC people were still being banished to remote areas of the country after serving their sentences. Some of these were Mlamli Makwetu, Selby Ngendane, Zephania Mothopeng and others. It was an attempt by the government to 'break the back of Poqo'. In fact, a South African publication reported that during February 1968, Mteteli Ntuli (an advocate) and Leonard Zambodla were sentencecd to death for the murder of a man regarded by them as a traitor.[2] In the middle of 1968 in widely scattered areas of Oudshoorn, Lainsburg, Graaff Reinet and Victoria West, several Africans were arrested for furthering the aims of a banned organization: POQO/PAC. A *Survey of Race Relations in South Africa reporting* about the arrests in Victoria West said:

Twenty six Africans and Coloured men were arrested in Victoria West at the end of April on charges of having conspired with one another and with 65 others to commit sabotage. Evidence was given in court that they planned to storm the police station, to murder policemen and steal weapons, to steal poisons and poison the town's drinking water, to cut the electricity supply and telephone call lines. During November ten of them were gaoled for three years each for having belonged to POQO and furthered its aims. Trials of others are proceeding.[3]

Another group of Poqo militants appeared in the Supreme Court in Grahamstown in June 1969. They had been arrested in Graaff Reinet. On the 2 July 1969, the *Star* in Johannesburg carried this news headline. *Death Sentence Next Time: Chief Justice Warns 24 PAC*. Then the paper went on to say:

A warning that if, in future people were brought before him and were convicted of carrying out the terrible aims of Poqo organization with violence he would not hesitate to impose the death sentence, was given by the Judge President, Mr. Justice Jennet, at the conclusion of the Poqo trial in the Supreme Court here.

The Judge told the accused that many Poqo cases had come before the courts during the past eight years and he sentenced them to prison terms ranging form 3 to 20 years. The Judge remarked that he was amazed that men of such calibre as some of those before him, school teachers and church elders, should have been foolish enough to allow themselves to be persuaded to join the PAC. Refuting the accused, the Judge said that it did not fall within the function of the Court to discuss the rights and wrongs of the living conditions of the black people in South Africa. His duty was to enforce the law.

It seems that the 1968 arrests in Victoria West, Graaff Reinet and other areas were connected with the infiltration of PAC through Mozambique. On the 2 July 1968 the *Star's Africa News Service* reported that

> Portuguese security forces were caught in a murderous cross-fire as they charged fleeing members of the Pan Africanist Congress of South Africa, according to first-on-the-spot account of the action in which three policemen were killed near Villa Pery last week.
>
> Chief Police Officer Manual Martins de souse led his men, including two members of the secret police, Pide, in a charge across the clearing. At that point a terrorist (freedom fighter and member of the Azania Peoples Liberation Army) hiding in ambush at the top of an escarpment opened fire from the right.
>
> Police Officer Eusebio Gonclaves Nobre (31) and Emidio Lopes Noguera (26), a Pide Officer, fell mortally wounded only 15 feet from the terrorists they were charging. African Police Constable Antonio Azarias Chieavane (30) was riddled with bullets.

POQO has proved difficult to crush and instead the years have brought experience. One observer has said, 'Poqo seems to be in South Africa for ever, at least until liberation.'

In fact, in 1970 the settler government was deeply worried by Poqo. This time the cause of worry was the PAC radio broadcasts from Radio Tanzania. The Minister of Posts and Telegraphs, Mr M.C. van Rensburg disclosed that the broadcasts were reaching South Africa. He warned Hertzog who had broken away from Vorster's Nationalist Party to re-join the ruling party. He drew his attention to the fact that the Pan Africanist Congress which was calling South Africa, Azania was happy about the split among the Europeans.

The Windhoek Advertiser 2 March 1970 quoted van Rensburg under the headlines: *Terrorists Broadcast Refers to H.N.P.* (This was Hert-zog's Herstigte Nationale Party—the ultra-right splinter from the Neo-Nazi ruling Nationalist Party). The paper reported van Rensburg as saying the PAC broadcast had said:

> The fact of the matter is that the Nationalist Party is seriously divided, and revolutionaries must take advantage of this situation. On to the peoples' war in Azania... On to victory and the total take-over of political power.
>
> The minister commented that Azania was the terrorist name for South Africa and said that the PAC broadcast had said that the split in the Nationalist Party was a wound that must not be allowed to heal and must be exploited by the terrorists.[4]

References:
1. *The Star*, 4 August 1964
2. 1968, *A survey of Race Relations in South Africa* pp 59.
3. *Ibid*.
4. *The Windhoek Advertiser*, 2 March 1970.

13. The Communist Party of South Africa

The Communist Party of South Africa was founded in 1921. Communist papers like the *Guardian* published in the 1930s and banned in 1954, assumed the names *Clarion*, *Advance*, *New Age*, and finally *Spark*. As a result of the government bans these papers contributed to the struggle in South Africa greatly. They kept people informed. The Communist Party of South Africa was also responsible for the 1946 mine strike in Johannesburg. Like white Liberals and 'sympathetic' whites the Communist Party of South Africa opposed apartheid, but all believed in 'leading' the Africans. Therefore, instead of organizing and educating the white setlers to support the African Revolution, the liberals and the 'communists' spent their time and energy recruiting Africans into their white minority parties. There would have been nothing wrong with this if the Africans had had the franchise. But they did not; and could never oust the minority apartheid settler government through constitutional means.

This approach to the struggle by liberals and white communists in South Africa could only blunt the militancy of the oppressed Africans. The South African Communist Party's collaboration with the settler government in serving as 'Native Representatives' in parliament, Sydney Bunting and Sam Khan, has already been examined.

Actions of this nature only helped to disqualify the Communist Party of South Africa as a revolutionary force determined to wage a revolutionary struggle. Its leaders denounced the violence of the oppressed against the violence of the oppressors as 'terrorism'. They also persued a policy of destroying all indigenous political parties or trade unions which refused to be controlled by them.

In his book, *The Awakening of the People*, I. Tabata of the Unity Movement of South Africa claimed that the Communist Party of South Africa can never tolerate any organization which it cannot control. In 1919 there emerged in South Africa a powerful African trade union, the Industrial and Commercial Union (ICU) led by Clements Kadalie.

It was so strong and influential that it was often said the settlers feared it more than they had feared Dingane. The ICU was weakened by the Communist Party of South Africa when Kadalie had refused them the right to dominate and interfere with his Union, the CPSA infiltrated and split ICU into two wings, finally completely destroyed it.

Jordan K. Ngubane offers the following insight into the Communist Party of South Africa:

> In 1929 Communism ceased to want a mass movement of its own. Instead the party was to remain the 'brains' of the liberation movement as a whole. Today, however, this circumstance places Communism in a position of relative weakness since its limited numbers make it impossible for it to take a clearly defined party stand or adopt an independent political programme. But this it could not do even before the enactment of Suppression of Communism Act, and to be effective at all it had, to *use* African political organizations as hosts.[1]

Of course, Jordan K. Ngubane is wrong to equate the Communist Party of South Africa with Communism.

The Sabotaging Role of the Communist Party of South Africa

The white reformist Communist Party of South Africa, under the disguise of the Congress of Democrats, has been the greatest saboteur of the liberation movement both within and outside south Africa. Two years before Sir Seretse Khama founded the Bechuanaland Democratic Party (in Botswana) the British Protectorate, as it was, already had a powerful party, the Bechuanaland Peoples' Party led by Matante, Motsete and Mpho, the Secretary. In Johannesburg Mpho was believed to be a sympathiser of the reformist South African Communist Party. Through him the white 'communists' wanted to act as the 'brains' of the liberation movement in Botswana. When they did not succeed they published statements issued by Mpho, without consent of the Party's executive committee, in *New Age*. This caused friction within the Bechuanaland Peoples' Party. It was clear that the 'brains' of the liberation movement were attempting to destroy the BPP if they could not control it through Mpho. The Party soon split into two wings, and later a third was formed. Mpho formed his own party with the financial support, probably from the Communist Party of South Africa. During the Botswana elections between 1964 and 1970, Mpho and his colleagues won only one seat.

Philip Matante's party which the reformist Communist Party of South Africa had tried to destroy, though weakened, succeeded in becoming the opposition to Sir Seretse Khama's ruling Party.

In Swaziland the Communist Party of South Africa sabotaged the struggle for freedom there under the progressive Ngwane National Liberation Congress. They infiltrated the Congress whose leading members were the President Dr Ambrose Zwane, the Vice-President MacDonald Maseko and Dumisa Dlamini, the Secretary-General. The Communist Party of South Africa wanted Mr Maseko as leader of the Ngwane National Liberation Congress for in him they saw their chance of assuming the role of 'brains' of the Swazi national struggle. The Ngwane National Liberation Congress was aligned to both Dr Kwame Nkruman's Ghana and the Pan Africanist Congress. The Communist Party of South Africa believed Maseko could achieve an alignment with the ANC.

South African Communist Party interference resulted in a protracted struggle for the leadership of the Ngwane National Liberation Congress, which enormously weakened it. The traditionalists seized this opportunity to organize the Imbokodo Party. At the 1965 elections it won all the seats! The Ngwane National Liberation Congress which had been expected to form the first government of an independent Swaziland failed to win a single seat. Dr Zwane's refusal to be controlled by the Communist Party of South Africa, had brought about his destruction.

The sabotaging role of the Communist Party of South Africa was also exerted in the British Colony of Basutoland. When Ntsu Mokhehle, President of the Basutoland Congress Party refused to be dictated to by the Moscow-oriented South African Communist Party, they tried to destroy him through their paper *New Age*. When this failed they formed the Communist Party of Lesotho. This party failed to win any support, and the action of the CPSA only served to militate against the establishment of a progressive government in an independent Lesotho.

In the 1965 elections the Basutoland Congress Party which had been expected to win and form the first government of an independent Lesotho, was defeated by the narrow margin of one seat, by Chief Leabua Jonathan. The CPSA had succeeded in weakening the Basutoland Congress Party, allowing the Basuto National Party to capitalize on the situation. In 1970, after losing the second general elections to Mokhehle's Basutoland Congress Party, Jonathan staged a coup d'etat, arrested Mokhehle and exiled King Moshoeshoe II to Holland.

The South West Africa Peoples' Organisation and the South West

Africa National Union. In the beginning the SWANU influenced by the Communist Party of South Africa worked with the African National Congress. The Pan Africanist Congress helped SWAPO and both organizations worked together. SWAPO was labeled 'reactionary' and SWANU 'revolutionary'.

The African National Congress Betrayed

The African National Congress of South Africa has itself been betrayed by the South African Communist Party. The most recent case is that of Nelson Mandela. In 1962 news leaked claimed that Nelson Mandela had said that the PAC stand was correct. He was also said to be planning to see Chief Luthuli to ask him to review the ANC policy of non-violence and adopt the nationalist approach to the struggle in South Africa. Some of the white 'communists' who attended this meeting in Basutoland (now Lesotho), accused him of 'selling out' to black chauvinism and warned him that his actions would result in serious trouble.

A week later, near Howick in Natal, Mandela who had been evading the police for months was arrested by the special branch chief, Spengler from Johannesburg.

It was also on the ill-advice of the leaders of the Communist Party of South Africa that Rivonia was discovered by the Boers in July 1963. At the time PAC members were being rounded up and ruthlessly persecuted by the government. The reformist white communists who had always feared the militancy of the PAC advised Mr Walter Sisulu to make a radio broadcast from their private station at Lilliessleaf Farm in Rivonia.

Immediately after the broadcast there were newspaper reports that Sisulu had broadcast a message from Ghana; then the rumours suggested Botswana. To everyone's dismay in the African community, newspapers then reported the arrest of Walter Sisulu and others on a 'white' farm in Johannesburg! Arthur Goldreich and Harold Wolpe the 'brains' of the African 'liberation' movement who had planned 'Operation Mayibuye' with Sisulu, managed to break out of their cell in Johannesburg, leaving their black 'colleagues' behind. They fled to Swaziland, and then flew to Botswana. In Botswana, Goldreich and Wolpe asked to be jailed because they were afraid they would be kidnapped.

Besides sabotaging the struggle South African Communist Party leadership has never shown any revolutionary courage. For instance, in 1964 Piet Byleveld, President of the Congress of Democrats and executive member of the Communist Party of South Africa gave evidence for the state during one of the trials. He said he could not sacrifice his 'personal liberty'. Yet another leading white member of the CPSA, Gerald Ludi turned out to be a spy. After his trip to Moscow he confessed that he was Vorster's agent, No QO18 and had been trained as an informer.

Some credit to the CPSA

To the South African Communist Party's credit, they have always given fantastic sums of money to organizations or leaders they supported and controlled. In South Africa Walter Sisulu's bail of £3,000 was paid by the Communist Party of South Africa. Abraham Fischer's bail of £5,000 was also paid by the CPSA. In 1969 the Survey of Race Relations reported that a sum of £1,000,000 had been given to the ANC by Russia through the CPSA.

However, political parties which refused to compromise on the fundamental question of repossession of the land and the right of Azanians to self-determination have had a very rough treatment at the hands of the Communist Party of South Africa. They have used vast sums of money to misinterpret and misrepresent African political organizations which refused to accept their line. They have always tried to suppress the activities of such organizations. As a result papers like *The African Communist*, and the British Anti-Apartheid *News*, published in London, rarely report Pan Africanist Congress activities unless distorted. *SOUTH AFRICA: The Struggle for a Birthright* by Mary Benson, and *The Rise of South African Reich* by Brian Bunting reflect this bias against organizations not influenced or controlled by white liberals or 'communists'.

In the early 1960s many CPSA members fled South Africa and found positions in international organizations which helped the 'apartheid struggle', they have detrimentally influenced organizations like the British Anti-Apartheid Movement and the Defence and Aid Fund. In 1963, when the PAC members in South Africa were faced with sabotage charges and other serious political offences, the spokesman for the Defence and Aid Fund in Johannesburg said that his organization could not defend people charged with sabotage. They would defend only those who were charged with lesser political offences. But when in July 1963 the leaders of the ANC were arrested the Defence and Aid Fund in Johannesburg reversed their position. But it was too late for the PAC men who had already been sentenced to long prison terms or death, without having received financial support for their legal expenses.

Condemning the CPSA's activities and influence, a spokesman for the Unity Movement of South Africa has said,

> The enormity of the crime committed by the liberals and Communist Party against the oppressed people of South Africa is to be seen in their role outside South Africa. They deliberately conceal the real struggle for liberation with the express purpose of smothering it, while at the same time they mount a vast anti-apartheid campaign to win the support of well-meaning people all over the world. ...In terms of the South African set up, anti-apartheid means anti-Afrikaner nationalist Government. It means the return to power of the English sections... the exploitation of the Black population.[2]

What are the facts of the PAC/ANC split?

The PAC did not break away from the ANC because the former were 'racialists' who were against racial co-operation. The 1949 programme of action rejected all forms of white leadership. Experience had already taught the African people that white leadership militated against their genuine interests.

With regard to the 'racialism' of PAC, *Africa and the World* of March 1965 asked this question: 'Is Sobukwe a Racialist?' The paper replied:

> In the view of *Africa and the World*, Sobukwe is revealed not as a racialist but as a realist, who understands that peace can only be built in South Africa (as anywhere else in the world) by the total rejection of all racialistic concepts. This means straight majority rule with no compromise with anything less.
>
> His slogan 'Africa for Africans' embraces *all* who genuinely owe their loyalty to Africa—a free Africa in which 'colour will count for nothing'—but his insistence that the pressure for change must come primarily from the most under-privileged, that is the Africans, is basic to all revolutionary philosophy, just as in Europe the pressure for social revolutionary change comes primarily from the working class.
>
> In such a process it is not possible to have a foot in two camps. Those who are not totally committed impede the revolution.

Outlining the case for his PAC, Mangaliso Sobukwe had himself said,

> It is our contention that the vast illiterate and semi-literate masses of the Africans are the cornerstone, the key and very life of the struggle for democracy. From this we draw the logical conclusion that the rousing and consolidation of the masses is the primary task of liberation.
>
> This leads to the conclusion that African Nationalism is the liberatory outlook to achieve this gigantic task and that the philosophy of Africanism holds out the hope of a genuine democracy beyond the stormy sea of struggle.
>
> We have made our stand clear on this point. Our contention is that the Africans are the only people who, because of their material position, can be interested in the complete overhaul of the present structure of society.
>
> We have admitted that there are Europeans who are intellectual converts to the African cause, but because they benefit materially from the present setup, they cannot completely identify themselves with that cause.
>
> Thus it is, as South African history so ably illustrates, that whenever Europeans 'co-operate' with African movements, they keep on demanding checks and counter-checks, guarantees and the like, with the result that they stultify and retard the movement of the Africans and the reason is, of course, that they are consciously or unconsciously protecting their sectional interests.
>
> *We do not wish to use anybody, nor do we intend to be used by anybody.* We want to *make the African people conscious of the fact that they have to win their own liberation*, rely on themselves to carry on a relentless and determined struggle instead of relying on court cases and negotiations on their behalf by 'sympathetic' whites.'

Speaking about Indians whose leadership was drawn from the merchant class of the South African Indian Congress, Sobukwe had said:

> The only Indians who can, because of their material position, be interested in the complete overthrow of white domination and the establishment of a genuine Africanist socialist democracy, are the poor 'coolies' of the sugar plantations of Natal. But they have not yet produced the leadership of their own...

To the African people this was realism to the settlers it was 'racialism'. This PAC stand, however, was adopted by university students in Azania and those at the University of Zambia in 1970.

On 29 August 1970 *The Times of Zambia* reporting on the new black student union, which had just broken from the white South African student union (NUSAS), said:

Black and Coloured university students in South Africa have set up their own union—because existing organiztations are white dominated.

And already, reports say that more than half of the 4,000 students eligible to join are members of the new union— South African Students Organization. The decision to form SASO was based on a four point arguement which included:
- Black students owe their first allegiance to the black community with whom they share burdens and injustices of apartheid.
- It is essential for the black students to strive to elevate the level of consciousness of the black community by promoting awareness, pride, achievement and capabilities...

The new body adopted policies on several subjects at a recent meeting. The view was expressed that silence in the face of injustice is tantamount to acceptance, thus SASO could not escape the obligation to protest...

But the consensus was that the involvement of black students in protests and public demonstration was to be viewed with reservations especially where black student interests were not directly involved.

On the 17 October 1970 the Zambia *Daily Mail* reported that a new student movement for the liberation of Southern Africa, SMOLISA had been formed at the University of Zambia. SMOLISA declared that it would accept only 'black revolutionary and progressive' students and involve them in the struggle against racism, imperialism and colonialism. The publicity secretary of the University of Zambia Students Union said that Coloured students who identified themselves with black people's cause would also be accepted but not those who aspired to be White.

He pointed out that this did not mean that SMOLISA was racialistic but was only being realistic about the situation created by the racists in the South and that it did not reflect Zambia's national policy.

The Communist Party of South Africa, read 'racialism' into the PAC stand, announced in April 1959. By 1970 many people had grown to distinguish between 'racialism' and 'realism' and there was no open protest or opposition from the South African Communist Party.

Domination of ANC by minority groups

As for the Congress Alliance, the African majority was dominated by a minority under the cloak 'multi-racialism'. These minorities included white South African Communists. The Youth League, under Dr Antony Muziwakhe Lembede's leadership had already rejected domination from *any* white minority group.

Communism was not the issue at all for, Chief Albert Luthuli, President General of the African National Congress had said, 'For myself I am not a communist. Communism seems to me to be a mixture of a false theory of society linked to a false 'religion'.'[3] At the 1957 Treason Trial, in which he was acquitted along with all the other ANC leaders, Chief Luthuli said, 'It is not Congress (ANC) policy to do away with private ownership or the means of production.'

For his part Nelson Mandela said,

As far as the Communist Party is concerned, and if I understand its policy correctly, it stands for the establishment of a state based on the principles of Marxism. The Communist Party's main aim, on the other hand, was to remove the capitalists and to replace them with a working class while the ANC seeks to harmonize them. This is a vital distinction...

From my reading of Marxist literature and from conversations with Marxists, I have gained the impression that communists regard the parliamentary system of the West as undemocratic and reactionary. But, on the contrary, I am an admirer of such a system.

The Magna Charta, the Petition of Rights and the Bill of Rights are documents which are held in veneration by democrats throughout the world.

I have great respect for British Parliament as the most democratic institution in the world, and the independence and impartiality of its judiciary never fail to arouse my admiration.

The American Congress, that country's doctrine of separation of power, as well as the independence of its judiciary, arouse in me similar sentiments... For several years an old friend with whom I worked very closely on the ANC and the Communist Party, had been trying to get me to join the Communist Party. I had many debates with him on the role which the Communist Party can play at this stage of our struggle, and I advanced to him the same views in regard to my political beliefs which I have described earlier in my statement.

In order to convince me that I should join the Communist Party, he from time to time gave me Marxist literature to read, though I did not always find time to do this.

Each of us always stuck to our guns in our arguments as to whether I should join the Communist Party...[4]

One of the chief supporters of the so-called 'Freedom' Charter, Bishop Desmon Tutu is recorded as saying, 'Surely you must see that *apartheid* is wholly un-Christian and totally evil... just as Nazism and Communism...'[5]

Mangaliso Robert Sobukwe first President of the Pan Africanist Congress said at the inaugral congress of the Party on 6 April 1959.

We are not blind to the fact that nations with a planned state economy have outstripped, in industrial development, those that follow the path of private enterprise. Today, China is industrially ahead of India... We also reject economic exploitation of the many for the benefit of a few... We accept as a policy the equitable distribution of wealth aiming, as far as I am concerned, to equality of income...[6]

A.P. Mda an Azanian ideologue associated with the Pan Africanist Congress saw the triumph of progressive African Nationalism resulting in the 'full political control by workers, peasants and revolutionary intellectuals and the liquidation of capitalism.'[7]

The PAC policies are based on the 1949 Programme of Action of nation-building. This programme was initiated by political leaders like Anton M. Lembede, Mangaliso R. Sobukwe, A.P. Mda, Zeph Mothopeng, Nyati Pokela. The 1949 Programme of Action was founded on progressive African Nationalism, socialism and democracy. Nationalism demands that the interests of the indigenous peoples should dominate over those of settlers and aliens. Socialism demands that the interests of the workers should be paramount in the control of the economy because the role of workers in the creation of wealth is more important than that of capital. Democracy demands that the interests of the majority must prevail over those of the minority.

From its inception, the PAC opted for an Africanist *socialist* democracy. Some PAC leaders and members feel that socialism for the PAC means the common or public ownership of the means of production, distribution and exchange such as the land, mineral resources, industry, commerce, finance and banking as distinct from nationalization of certain enterprises in a mixed economy in which there are both private and public sectors, or the nationalization of all enterprises as in State capitalism which prevails in some socialist countries of Eastern Europe. These leaders and members argued that in an Africanist socialist democracy, people will be free to use their skills and talents and pursue a livelihood by all legitimate means except exploitation of other people either directly through appropriation of the surplus labour power, or indirectly through manipulation of the commodity market.

This socialism is Africanist not only in the sense that it will be scientific socialism adapted to African conditions, but also in the deeper sense that it draws its inspiration from African traditions. This African heritage has in large measure been dissipated by Western colonialism and imperialism. The idea is to salvage what is left of it and reinforce it with modern socialist ideas and adapt it to present-day needs. A PAC member has remarked, 'This is one of several ways in which we can talk meaningfully of scientific socialism.'

PAC did not leave the ANC because of 'Communism', as the ANC was never 'communist'. The PAC is for the restoration of the Azanian land to its owners and its wealth to the Azanians. Of course, the immediate goal is the waging of the national democratic revolution—then socialism.

Even Winnie Mandela subscribes to this view. In August 1976, she was asked, 'Is Black Consciousness Movement the vehicle for change in South Africa?' According to *National Mirror* of Zambia, she replied,

> There is no other solution. Blacks have to speak for Blacks and develop self-reliance and pride. Nevertheless, what we are witnessing now cannot be necessarily attributed to the Black Consciousness Movement. The issues are more those of a Black nation versus a white minority.

In South Africa, race is class and class race

There are many people including socialists who often wonder why the white workers do not join with the Black workers and wage a 'class struggle' in South Africa. In an open letter to No Sizwe, author of *One Azania One Nation*, A. Sivanandan of the Institute of Race Relations in London when questioning some of No Sizwe's points on race and class and nation in South Africa, raised some intresting issues:

'South Africa was a settler society which neither assimilated itself into the indigenous social structure (as Aryan India) nor was able to decimate the native population (as in the USA or the Caribbean),' pointed out Sivanandan. 'The settlers instead were (and are) a slender minority, distinguished by race and colour, faced with a massive black population (the only parallel is Zimbabwe) hence, the only way they could preserve their economic privileges and their political power was to stand full-square against the encroachments of the black masses.'

He alleged that the struggle in South Africa was a class struggle to be waged by the working class as a whole, black and white. But he pointed out that in South Africa class is race and race is class. He said that as long as the blacks

> are forced to remain a race apart, the white working class can never become a class for itself. And as for blacks, if the unending rebellion of the past few years and birth of the Black Consciousness Movement are anything to go by, they are fast becoming both a race and a class for themselves—and that is a formidable warhead of liberation...[8]

In fact, in 1979 white workers in a South African gold mine went on a strike as a demonstration of their unrelenting opposition to three Coloureds who were being promoted to do skilled work, traditionally reserved for Whites. The white working class in South Africa suffers from racial arrogance and has a fascist attitude toward the black working class. The white working class can only be liberated by a revolution. It seems they will be 'class brothers' of the black working class only after the revolution. The revolution should not wait for them to make up their minds. They have already been given enough time.

In his New Year Message to the Azanian Nation on the 31 December 1982, the PAC leader, Nyati Pokela said

> ...the elimination and liquidation of apartheid must be coupled at every stage with the restoration of the inalienable rights of our people to their land.
>
> One example should suffice to strengthen our reasoning. In this connection the Algerian case for independence from French

colonialism is instructive in that during that period also deceptive
tendencies arose to argue that Algeria was an extension of
France. In truth even some well-known progressives in France
and Algeria regarded Algerian demands as 'separatist'. Indeed,
they called for a class war of Algeria and French workers
against the French bourgeoisie. They ignored an important
point and fact, that Algeria had a history and a past and its
people were not French, but colonized subjects. In this case the
will of the people, the will of the colonised triumphed. And
through their own efforts discriminatory laws were ended...

The numerical superiority of the Africans

The PAC unlike the ANC believed in Black leadership and self-reliance.
Of course, the white settlers called this tendency 'racism' or 'go it alone
tendency'. The whites have never reconciled themselves to African in-
itiative. They have always believed that the African belongs to the 'child
race' and must be led and guided to 'adulthood' by Whites.

This view influenced the ANC leadership. They held that South
Africa was a 'unique' situation. Professor Z.K. Matthews, for instance,
said in 1957,

> South Africa differs from other territories in Africa such as
> Ghana or Nigeria or even Uganda where the black man out-
> numbers the white man to such an extent that it is ridiculous to
> talk about the country being anything other than black man's
> country. In South Africa in addition to the African we have
> settled here significant numbers of other groups. Europeans,
> Asians and Coloureds—and therefore the country must be
> recognized as a multi-racial country with all that it implies.[9]

This view is forcefully countered by a group of Azanian Marxists who
in 1980; aptly put it:

> The Africans of Azania are the indigenous inhabitants, the
> natives of Azania; and they constitute the overwhelming
> majority of the entire population. They are natives, original
> owners of the country, who were robbed of it and its natural
> wealth, along with their livelihood by European colonialism.
> The colonial conquest which triumphed 300 years ago over
> heroic resistance, and broke it at the end of the 19th century by

sheer weight of Europe's advanced (military) technology which
was then unkown to Africa, subsequently subjected the Africans
to three huge mountains that weigh heavily on them: ruthless
political subjugation, whose chief characteristic is the African's
lack of any constitutional means of political redress, resistance
of self-defence, since white domination does not regard them as
citizens and disallows their representation in any state organ.
Unparalelled economic exploitation by both settler and capital
(apartheid's business) and western imperialism (big business)...
Africans (are)... the most oppressed population group in their
fatherland. The Africans want to fully an manifestly assume the
effective control of their country. In a word, to recapture it
form foreign rule and then govern it in the best and true interests of all who shall continue to inhabit it as full-blooded
members of the new Azanian nation. Therefore the Africans
constitute the core of the nation.

Historically the Asians have no territory of their own in
Azania, and they have never made any forceful claims on any
piece of land in the country. Herein lies the difference between
them and the European invaders. The plight of the Asians is the
same as that of the dispossessed Africans... Coloureds are *not* a
foreign group.

The minority whites in Azania have no territory of their
own in the country, nor any rightful claim to any part of it.
Their political supremacy, a necessary outcome of thier colonial
conquest, as well as their absolute monopoly of the effective
instruments of power, has not and never can change the
axiomatic truth.[10]

The Independent Black Republic Thesis of 1928

The Independent Black Republic Thesis on Azania (South Africa) was
first proposed by the Executive Committee of the Communist International in November 1928, at the Sixth World Congress. This thesis
is in accord with the wars of national resistance and the 1949 programme
of action. A number of resolutions on the National and Colonial Question were adopted by the Congress.

The Sixth World Congress resolved that

South Africa is a British dominion of the Colonial type. The development of relations of capitalist production has led to British imperialism carrying out the economic exploitation of the country with the participation of the white bourgeoisie of South Africa (British and Boers). Of course, this does not alter the general colonial character of the economy of South Africa, since the British capital continues to occupy the principal economic position in the country (banks, mining and industry) and since the South African bourgeoisie is equally interested in the mercantile exploitation of the Negro population.

In the recent period in South Africa we have witnessed the growth of the manufacturing, iron and steel industries, the development of commercial crops (cotton and sugar cane) and the growth of capitalist relations in agriculture, chiefly in cattle raising. On the basis of this growth of capitalism there is chiefly a growing tendency to expropriate the land from the Negroes and from a certain section of the white farming population. The South African bourgeoisie is endeavouring also by legislature, means to create a cheap market of labour power and a reserve army.

The overwhelming majority of the population is made up of Negroes (Black people) and Coloured people (about 5,500,000 Negroes and Coloured people) and about 1,500,000 White people, according to the 1921 census.

A characteristic feature of the colonial type of the country is the almost complete landlessness of the Negro population: the Negroes hold only one eigth of the land, whilst seven-eights of the land have been expropriated by the white population. There is no Negro bourgeoisie as a class, apart from the individual Negroes engaged in trading and a thin strata of Negro intellectuals who do not play any essential role in the economic and political life of the country.

The Negroes constitute also the majority of the working class: ...Another characteristic of the proletarization of the native population is the fact that the number of black workers grows faster than the number of white workers. Another characteristic feature is the great difference in the wages and material conditions of the white and black proletariat in general. The great disproportion between the wages of white and black proleteriat continues to exist as the characteristic feature of the colonial type of the country...

The Communist Party (of South Africa) must orientate itself chiefly on the national question in colonial matters.

In replying to the *Independent Black Republic Thesis*, the South African Communist Party delegation leader, Sydney Bunting said:

In an earlier debate, I ventured the opinion, that it might be universally true, that the chief function of a colonial people was to engage in a national struggle (predominantly agrarian in character) against the foreign imperialism and for independence. and that in South Africa at any rate, the class struggle of the proletariat appeared more capable of accomplishing the same task.

But this task is no longer so easy. It is no longer a mere case of the national and class movements coinciding as it were automatically. Here the Whites exploited are of the very race against which the natives exploited as nationalists are fighting. It is almost inevitable that *the nationalist movement of the natives will clash with their class movement*. Similarly, the white exploited, finding their race being attacked as such by a native nationalist movement, are predisposed by their superior economic and political position to *side with their master national and forget their class struggle...*

The delegation of the White Communist Party of South Africa was not happy with the arguments put forward as the Black Independent Republic Thesis. They claimed that expressions like 'South Africa is a black country', 'the return of the country and the land to the native population,' and so forth though correct as general statements, invite criticism by the working class and peasant minority. The 'native republic' is defended, indeed, as a mere expression of majority-rule, but it obviously goes beyond that. And the little difference makes all the difference. It handicaps propaganda, when it comes to combatting white chauvisnism.

In opposing the right of Azanains to self-determination, the South African 'Communist' delegation, Sydeny Bunting also argued that 'South Africa is a Whiteman's country, where whites can and do live not merely as planters and officials but as a whole nation of all classes, established there for three centuries of Dutch and English composition.'

Bunting's wife, another leading South African communist went further for she argued that the land of South Africa had never really belonged to the Blacks in the first place, since according to her understanding the Boers and Blacks arrived in the area at the same time and were both equally responsible for driving the original inhabitants out of the area.

Her real concern, and those of her 'communist' colleagues was revealed when she asked: 'Who will guarantee equality for the Whites in an independent native republic? Their slogan as you know is 'drive the Whites to the sea!'[11]

Communist International replies Bunting

In its Resolution the Polit Secretariat of the Executive Committee of the Communist International said among other things:

At the meeting of the Polit Secretariat of the ECCI of October 1928, among other things, the South African question was dealt with and a corresponding resolution adopted.

The South African question has already played an important role in the discussions of the Sixth World Congress, both in the colonial and in the Negro question. Proceeding from these discussions and former resolutions of the ECCI it was only necessary to establish the tasks of the Communist Party of South Africa.

A clear elaboration of the slogan which the CP of South Africa has to take up the fight, was the more necessary as just in this regard the majority of the Central Committee of the South African Communist Party represented a view deviating from that of the Executive and also of the 6th World Congress. The main slogan of an independent South African Republic of natives. In regard to this slogan Comrade Bunting (South Africa) declared in his speech at the Sixth World Congress in the discussion on the colonial question that this formulation is combatted by the majority of the CP of South Africa chiefly for practical reasons.

It is clear that the opinion, as represented by the majority of the CP of South Africa, shows a lack of understanding for the tasks of our Party regarding the revolutionary struggle of the native masses. This is precisely the reason for the weak influence of our Party upon the native masses in spite of the objectively favourable circumstances...

The Executive Committee of the Communist International said that there was no question of subordinating the struggle of the dispossessed and oppressed and exploited Africans to the whims of undecided workers.

The opposition to the Independent Black Republic Thesis by the Communist Party of South Africa angered African revolutionaries in the ANC, who formed another organization: in 1930 the Independent African National Congress was founded in the Western Cape. Bransby Ndobe and Elliot Tonjeni were its main leaders. The Independent ANC set out to build itself into a 'militant African liberation movement which will not bow to the knee to British and Boer Imperialism', it sought mass action to this end and adopted the slogan for the Independent Black Republic Thesis in Azania. But as one writer put it, 'the (settler) regime was not about to give it a chance. Both Ndobe and Tonjeni were banished... and the group soon collapsed.'[12]

A White 'Communist' calls for an independent Eritrea

Joe Slovo's wife was vice-president at the 'Permanent Tribunal of the Peoples Session on Eritrea', held in Manila in May 1980. Eritrea is considered part of Ethiopia under the Charter of the Organisation of African Unity.

Ruth First was a supporter of the 'Freedom' Charter which denied the Azanian people the right to self-determination. In her submission to the Tribunal she said:

> As a member of a national liberation movement of South Africa, the African National Congress, we are confronted with having to conduct a struggle which, like Eritrea, is fighting an enormous concentration of power which represses the rights of the people. And as far as I am concerned Eritrea is not a national question; it is an international question. And I would recognise it also as an international issue... The case of Eritrea is a unique case. It is a case of the infringement of territorial frontiers of a distinct country by an annexing power, Ethiopia.
>
> This evidence: the historical evidence, the social evidence, the political evidence of Eritrea as a distinct country—distinct from Ethiopia althouth they shared occupation for perhaps six years, and only six—this evidence, I repeat is of two peoples with the distinct histories of political struggle and distinct needs of *self-determination*.

Ruth First and her colleagues in the South African Communist Party have always feared self-determination in Azania. They feared the Independent Black Republic Thesis advocated by the Comintern. She may have been right in supporting the right of the Eritreans of self-determination, but then why oppose the right of self-determination in Azania!

A group of Azanian Marxists have put forward an explanation. They argued that:

> After World War I, and with the victory of the Russian October Revolution in 1917, a new era was ushered, the era of World Proletariat revolutions. It was at this stage that a false start was made in Azania. Once again, the White (privileged) workers took the initiative. Of course, this was not surprising since they were better exposed to world events, and they were freed from labour repression.
>
> In 1921, they formed the Communist Party of South Africa, which was *exclusively* White and Colonialist in orientation, so that while in other colonial and semi-colonial countries such as China (the Communist Party of China was formed in the same year), Korea, Vietnam, Albania etc., genuine Marxist-Leninist Parties were formed—ours was a *racist party* from the outset, no wonder that it has consistently (even when the majority of its members were black) followed and maintained an erroneous policy on the National Question. This was evidenced during the 1922 Rand Miners' Strike, where racist slogans were displayed, chief of which was 'Workers of the World Unite to fight for a White South Africa!'

I.B. Tabata on the 'Communist' Party of South Africa

I.B. Tabata, author of *Imperialsit Conspiracy in South Africa*, has written extensively on the South African Communist Party. The SACP he writes:

> is not concerned with discussing unity with the Pan Africanist Congress or with any other organisations in South Africa other than those it already controls... It is common knowledge that the African National Congress is not and cannot be a master of its own house. Even on the question of unity which is demanded by the OAU, it is not in a position to make up its own mind and take an independent decision.

The ANC abroad has long been an instrument of foreign policy of a big power because it depended heavily on it for financial support. It is not simply the largeness of the amounts of money donated but the method of making the support unavoidable that ensures control of the Congress. the monies come to the ANC via the Communist Party of South Africa.[13]

Tabata continues:

Our charge against the Communist Party of South Africa is that its members, especially the leadership which consists of white petit-bourgeois intellectuals, are nothing but radical liberals of the South African type, which means they are tainted in various degrees of racialism. This is why it is possible for them, in times of crisis to unite with the other dye-in-the-wool white liberals to save the system of segregation or apartheid, in short herren-volkism in South Africa.

Tabata also points at the number of White spies who have been found in the ANC ranks. He draws attention to the fact that during the Revonia Trial in 1964,

the police were in possession of an inordinate number of documents and a vast amount of information. The Congress Alliance was infiltrated by police spies that the man who kept the post office box key and collected the post every day was a white policeman seconded from the police force. It is he who identified the publications and gave evidence that many circulars were written by the Communist Party of South Africa and published in the name of the African National Congress. Among the documents produced were the Minutes of a meeting of what is called 'The Centre', the most authoritative body of the Communist Party of South Africa. The meeting was concerned with formulation of the policy to be presented to the Congress Alliance consisting of Democrats (COD), a group of white liberals, the African National Congress (ANC), the South African Indian Congress (SAIC), an Indian Organization dominated by the Indian merchant class; the Coloured Peoples Congress, a group created by the Communist Party to represent the Coloured People in Alliance.

One of the problems that confronted the CPSA was that its

protege, the ANC was being publicly accused of being a stooge organizatgion. Thus the minutes of 'the Centre' contain, inter alia, the following: 'A picture... has been taken advantage.. to depict the ANC as collaborationist organization dominated by non-Africans. It is essential that this picture be corrected... particularly in Free Africa... We ask all members (white liberals, merchant class Indian Congress etc)... to support this ruling.[14]

In 1980 a group of Whites arrived in Lusaka, Zambia. They were photographed with Mr Oliver Tambo at a press conference addressed by the ANC President. The four Whites claimed that they had escaped form jail in South Africa through the machinery of the ANC, and Umkonto Wesizwe. Some Zambians were surprised. One of them asked, 'How can the ANC help the Whites to escape when their own leader Nelson Mandela has been in jail for a long time, but they never did anything to help him escape?' The *Survey of Race Relations In South Africa* in Johannesburg soon revealed the reasons.

In January Messrs. Lee, Jenkins and Maumaris who escaped from Pretoria Central Prison in December said their escape had been assisted by the ANC, SA Communist Party and Umkonto Wesizwe. They denied that they had been assisted by prison officials. However, a prison warden Mr Francois Daniel Vermeulen was charged in February with having assisted them to escape.[15]

The International University Exchange Fund was rocked in 1979 by Craig Williamson. He had ingratiated himself with the Communist Party of South Africa and the African National Congress.

During the time of Craig Williamson, a campaign to have the OAU withdraw its recognition of the PAC was intensified by the ANC and the South African Communist Party. Spies like Craig Williamson also effectively sowed disunity within the OAU. It was in the South African Communist Party's interest to have the Pan Africanist Congress and the African National Congress at loggerheads. Johnston Mfanakithi Makhathini illustrates this well. He was the ANC representative at the United Nations in 1978 and astonished African and world diplomats in New York when he refused to participate in a United Nations meeting called to remember and honour the PAC President Mangaliso Sobukwe.[16]

The Tripoli Declaration of Heads of State and Government on the 26 November 1982 said

REITERATE our support for the just struggle waged by the people of South Africa for national liberation and call up all member states to give all forms of assistance to the national liberation movements recognised by the OAU (the African National Congress and the Pan Africanist Congress of Azania...

ANC leaders like Makhathini and Alfred Nzo were hostile towards the PAC because the PAC policies were in direct conflict with the neo-colonialist Freedom Charter which the liberals were promoting. The liberals themselves expressed concern at the growth and influence of the Pan Africanist Congress.

In *The Liberal Dilemma in South Africa*, the writer asserts in 1979

In view of the repression of both the African National Congress and the Pan Africanist Congress by the SA Government in the 1960s, it is difficult to say which of the two movements commands mass support, but the sporadic unrest of the 1970s and especially, the events of 1976 indicate considerable support for a black nationalism that would exclude Whites.[17]

However the Pan Africanist Congress of Azania as long ago as 1959 said, 'politically, we stand for the government of Africans by the Africans for the Africans, with *everybody* who owes his loyalty only to Africa and accept the democratic rule of an African majority, being regarded as an African...' White people have nothing to fear from the Pan Africanist Congress, for non-racialism is enshrined in the PAC constitution. No African country ever drove White settlers away after independence. Instead they were offered the citizenship of the new nation and asked to make their economic contribution. Azania will *not* drive away Whites.

The Liberal Dilemma In South Africa also said,

The hardening of black attitudes in the sixties heralded by new Africanist dissension in the ANC, the rise of the Pan Africanist Congress with its racial (for 'racial' read nationalist or revolutionary) appeal and on the student front, the establishment of exclusively black student organizations the African Students Association, the African Students of the Union of South Africa and later South African Students Organization (SASO) posed acute problems for the liberal intellectual whites.

Failure to appreciate what the PAC stands for by the liberals is probably the reason why they have promoted the Freedom Charter.

The complaint about the Freedom Charter

The 'Freedom Charter' which the Communist Party of South Africa helped to push forward in 1955 as a guideline for freedom in South Africa seems to have been unrealistic and intended to sabotage and confuse the Azanian revolution. The charter among other things said:

> There shall be equal status in the bodies of state, in the courts and in schools for all national groups and races;
> All national groups shall be protected by law against insult to thier race and national pride...

Here it seems the authors of the Freedom Charter did not believe in a free unified non-racial nation as elsewhere in Africa. But in a nation that still existed as Africans, Indians, Coloureds, English and Afrikaners.

At any event the charter was ill timed. It was proposed as the oppression of the Africans had been intensified by the newly elected Nationalist Party leader, Strydom in 1955.

Not long before he had made a speech to a cheering crowd of his settler followers. Among other things he had said:

> 'Waarop staan ek?' (Where am I standing!)
> 'Op die grond Meneer.' (on the ground, Sir), the cheering crowd had answered.
> 'Nee' (No), the Nazi-inspired Boer leader had retorted, 'Ek staan nie op die grond nie. Ek staan of die Kafir se nek' (I am not standing on the ground. I am standing on the Kaffir's neck).

To this there had been a maddening applause by the happy Boer settler supporters of the racist Nationalist Party.

In view of the growing repression it was not surprising when Chief Albert Luthuli said 'Congress did not unanimously adopt the Charter...'[18] The militant leadership of the African people was angered by the charter. Their spokesman said:

> Following the capture of a portion of the black leadership of South Africa by a section of the white ruling class, the masses of our people are in extreme danger of being deceived into losing sight of the objectives of our struggle. This captured leadership is fighting to perpetuate, the tutelage of the African people. It is fighting for the 'constitutional guartantees' or 'national

rights' for our alien nationals...

These 'leaders' consider South Africa and its wealth to belong to all who live in it, the alien dispossessors and the indigenous dispossessed, the alien robbers and their indigenous victims. They regard as equals the foreign master and his slave, the white exploiter and the African exploited, the foreign oppressor and the indigenous oppressed. They regard as brother the subject Africans and their European overlords. They are... naive, fantastically unrealistic to see that the interests of the subjected peoples who are criminally oppressed, ruthlessly exploited and inhumanly degraded, are in sharp conflict and in pointed contradiction with those of the white ruling class. Citizen Toussant once remarked that: 'Whenever anybody, be he white or mulatto, wants a dirty job done, he always gets a black man to do it.'

The Kliptown charter, which literally surrendered the land of the African people's land and wealth to Strydom, was described by another African leader as 'a colossal political fraud ever perpetrated upon the oppressed, exploited and degraded people. It clearly bears the imprint of its origin! It is a product of the slave mentality and colonialist orientation of the White middle classes of South Africa.' Quoting Sheik Karume of Zanzibar, he concluded, 'The land belongs to you (Africans). Whosoever tries to stop you seizing it, pours petrol over himself with one hand, and lights it with the other.'

Commenting on the 'Freedom' Charter, an African journalist deeply involved in the politics, wrote

The charter begins by repudiating the anti-colonialist slogan *Africa for Africans*, saying, 'South Africa belongs to all who live in it, Black and White', and then proceeds in abstract terms to blame a 'form of government' for robbing the people of their 'birthright'. It thus calculatingly conceals the embarrassing truth that the people have been robbed of their land not by a form of government but by the White oppressors.

The White people of South Africa, who constitute one-fifth of the population, occupy 87 per cent of the land surface. Scores of individual Whites own large tracts of farmland under freehold tenure. This has been effected through large scale usurpation of African land over a period of more than three centuries. Yet the charter now affirms their ownership of this land, since the country 'belongs' to them, too.

Under a policy of private ownership of land, such as is advocated in the charter, the people will be free to buy land where they wish. We are assured by the charterists that 'All shall have the right to occupy land wherever they choose' and that 'Restrictions on land ownership on a racial basis shall be ended.'

The writer also points out that

mere removal of restrictions on land ownership on a racial basis does not automatically make land available for sale. A mere declaration that a man is free to buy land wherever he chooses does not invest him with the wherewithal to pay for it. Even granting that the state would be in a position to raise the enormous sums that would be involved in a land-purchase and resettlement scheme, there is no guarantee that the White farmers would be willing to sell.

Viewed from any angle one chooses, the charter is nothing but a gigantic swindle. Under freehold tenure, those who at present fatten on the fat of our land, will, if the freedom charterists have their way, continue in effective occupation of the usurped land, while the vast majority of the people are offered freedom to starve, overcrowded and wallow in the slums of 13 per cent of the land.[19]

'The Pan Africanist Congress has started off with tremendous advantages ideologically, and has skillfully exploited opposition to the Whites and partnership'[20] Nelson Mandela entered in his diary in 1962. The Paris Declaration on the history of resistance in South Africa said

The apartheid regime is illegitimate and has no right to represent the people of South Africa. Such a regime is the byproduct of a White settler minority in 1910.

The international recognition of South Africa as a sovereign independent state has impeded the struggle for liberation in South Africa...[21]

The PAC approach to the liberation struggle in South Africa. Evidence increasingly vindicates their position.

African nationalism reactionary?

In Africa almost all colonized people won their freedom and independence through progressive African nationalism as a liberatory creed. This was because this force was more appealing than any other in pre-independent Africa. Indeed, nationalism has always been more relevant and effective in a national democratic revolution. It is of course true that in many countries the genuine revolution of the dispossessed people involving economic independence from imperialist countries was betrayed by nationalist leaders who continued the exploitative capitalist system of the over-thrown colonialists and imperialists. Instead of genuine independence where people control not only thier parliament but their country's wealth for the good of their own people; there emerged in certain African countries, so-called 'pro-western' countries which were nothing but semi-colonies of the imperialist powers in desguise. But this tragedy cannot be blamed on African Nationalism.

The Communist Party of South Africa failed to appreciate that in Azania, for true freedom and independence there are two phases to the struggle. First there is the struggle for the national democratic revolution which must involve every patriot. Success of this struggle is followed by the struggle for economic independence and freedom from imperialist exploitation. Perhaps it is fitting to mention what Chairman Mao Tse-tung has taught about the two-stage revolution. In December 1939 he said:

> we can see that the Chinese revolution taken as a whole involves a twofold task. That is to say, it embraces a revolution that is bourgeois-democratic in character (a new democratic revolution) and a revolution that is proletarian-socialist in character—it embraces the twofold task of revolution at both the present and the future stages.
>
> The leadership in this twofold revolutionary task rests on the shoulders of the party of the Chinese proletariat, the Chinese Communist Party, for without its leadership no revolution can succeed.
>
> To complete China's bourgeois-democratic revolution (the new democratic revolution) and to prepare to transform it into a socialist revolution when all necessary conditions are present—that is the sum total of the great and glorious revolutionary task of the Communist Party of China. All members of the Party should strive for its accomplishment and should never give up

half-way. Some immature Communists think that we have only the task of the democratic revolution at the present stage, but not that of the socialist revolution at the future stage; or that the present revolution or the agrarian revolution is in fact the socialist revolution. It must be emphatically pointed out that both views are erroneous. Every Communist must know that the whole Chinese revolutionary movement led by the Chinese Communist Party is a complete revolutionary movement embracing the two revolutionary stages, democratic and socialist, which are two revolutionary processes differing in character, and that the socialist stage can be reached only after the democratic stage is completed. The democratic revolution is the necessary preparation for the socialist revolution, and the socialist revolution is the inevitable trend of the democratic revolution... We can give correct leadership to the Chinese revolution only on the basis of a clear understanding of both the differences between the democratic and socialist revolution and their interconnections.[22]

References:
1. Jordan K. Ngubane, *An African Explains Apartheid*, p.182.
2. The Unity Movement of South Africa, *The Revolutionary Road for South Africa*, pp.17-18.
3. Albert Luthuli, *Let My People Go*, p.135.
4. Extracts from Nelson Mandela's trial held in the Old Synagogue Court, Pretoria 15 October to 7 November 1962.
5. South African Council of Churches, *Ecunews*, September 4 1981.
6. PAC, 'The Speeches of Mangaliso Robert Sobukwe', *Observer Mission to the United Nations*, New York, p.25.
7. Ernest Harsch, *South Africa—White Rule Black Revolt*, p.227, Monad Press, New York.
8. *Race and Class* Winter 1981 Volume XXII Number 3, pp.299-300
9. Z.K. Matthews, 'Non-White Political Organisations', *Africa Today*, as quoted in *Black Power in South Africa The Evolution of an Ideology*, by Gail Gerhart, p.205.
10. Statement by a group of Azanian Marxists.
11. *The Revolutionary Worker*, 2 October 1981, Chicago Illinois.
12. Ernest Harsch, *South Africa—White Rule Black Revolt*, p.208, Monad Press, New York.
13. I.B. Tabata, *Imperialist Conspiracy in South Africa*, p.123, Monad Press, New York.

14. *Ibid*, p.122.
15. *1981 Survey of Race Relations in South Africa*.
16. Peter Dreyer, *Martyrs and Fanatics—South Africa and Human Destiny*, p.134. Simon and Schuster, New York.
17. Pierre L. van Beghe (ed.), *The Liberal Dilemma in South Africa*, p.147, Croom Helm, London 1979.
18. *Albert Luthuli, Let My People Go*, p.160.
19. *The New African*, March 1967, Gransight Holdings Ltd, London.
20. *The New African*, March 1957, Gransight Holdings Ltd, London.
21. A report of the International Seminar on the 'History of Resistance Against Occupation, Oppression and Apartheid in South Africa', held at UNESCO House, Paris, 29 March, 2 April 1982.
22. *Selected Works of Mao Tse-Tung*, Volume three, pp.100-101, Lawrence & Wishart Ltd, London 1954.

14. The ANC Non-Violence and Dialogue

From the very beginning the ANC realized that the African people could never be the same again. That is, they could never survive in dignity and power as separate tribes. They were to be transformed into a mighty black nation. The ANC was to serve the interests of the natives of Azania. The ANC leaders therefore, organized the African people on a national basis. The Xhosas, the Zulus, the Sothos, the Vendas, the Shanganes and so on were to unite and form a new transformed nation rising out of the ashes of the defeated great heroes like Hintsa, Dingane, Moshoeshoe, Sekhukhuni and others.

To succeed, the ANC then had to overcome tribalism, and all tribes were to be given a sense of a common African nationhood. The presidents of the ANC as national leaders came from various tribes: Dr Dube was Zulu, Rev Mahabane was Sotho; Dr Xuma was Xhosa; Dr Moroka was Sotho and Chief Luthuli was Zulu. However these men were elected as national leaders on merit and not because of their tribe.

The African National Congress lit the torch of freedom not only for Africans in Azania but also for the people of Southern and Central Africa: Basutoland, Swaziland, Nyasaland (now Malawi) and Northern Rhodesia (now Zambia) formed their own Congresses to fight for freedom and independence. Congresses in these territories were founded as a result of students from these countries who went to Fort Hare University College in South Africa or workers who had gone to South Africa to seek employment.

The South African ANC is over seventy years old. It is regarded as the oldest political organization in Africa, but it has achieved little. It should be clear why the ANC failed. It abandoned the nationalist path and sought concessions instead of the right of the indigenous Africans to self-determination and national sovereignty.

The ANC was jolted in 1957 when its national speaker, R.V. Selope-Thema , a very popular ANC leader broke away to form what he called the nationalist minded block of the Congress. He advocated that the African people should struggle for self-determination just as other Africans were doing under colonial rule throughout Africa. He said that the ANC should not seek concessions from the white minority government but must fight for majority rule.

In his article 'Urban Revolt in South Africa: A case Study', Edward Feit says,

> Until 1944 the African National Congress had been largely an organisation of the African elite. It had confined its activities to attempts to work within the South African constitution, and to secure change by petitions and appeals. The change came after the Second World War. With the victory of the ANC Youth League in 1949, a more militant course was adopted. Militancy was, however, to be by demonstration only, and violence was expressly eschewed. Allying themselves with the South African Indian Congress, and later with a variety of other Congresses, each one of the main racial groups in the country, which together made up the Congress Alliance. They undertook a series of campaigns which, despite some spectacular demonstrations, proved abortive. In 1958 the momentum of the ANC seemed largely spent. The organization was split in two, with the more nationalist wing breaking away as the Pan Africanist Congress.[1]

The moderation of the ANC

The African National Congress was unquestionably an organiztation of very gentle people. They sincerely believed that they could gain concessions for their people through talk and non-violence. Mahatma Ghandi's philosophy of passive resistance and non-violence greatly influenced the ANC, particularly after India's independence in 1947. The ANC leaders failed to appreciate that the Indian situation and the settler situation in South Africa were different.

Writing about the ANC, a white university lecturer says, 'Reviewing the story of the ANC, it would seem that all times they were more concerned with non-violence against Whites than against their own people'.[2]

The ANC leaders did not accept the politics of majority rule. Talk about African majority rule was labelled 'racialism'. History was also avoided for it might generate 'racial hatred'. In reply to the historical distortions by Verwoerd and Eric Louw and the like, Chief Luthuli simply said, 'For us, questions of who came first to which part of South Africa, are irrelevant. The vital issue is not a squabble over the past, but the reality of today, and salvation in the present.'

Nelson Mandela confirms this.

I have already mentioned that I was one of the persons who helped to form Umkhonto. I, and others who started the organization, did so for two reasons... we believed that as a result of Government policy, violence by the African people had become inevitable, and that unless responsible leadership was given to canalize and control the feelings of our people, there would be outbreaks of terrorism which would produce an intensity of bitterness and hostility between the various races of this country which is not produced even by war, ...the violence which we chose to adopt was not terrorism. Those who formed Umkhonto were all members of the African National Congress, and had behind us the ANC tradition of non-violence.[3]

This policy of non-violence was consistent with the attitude of white liberals. It also brought praise from all quarters, including the settlers.

In July 1981, an article written by the white journalist Suzanne Cronje, appeared in the *New African*, 'Guerrillas Who Display An Unusual Touch of Humanity'.

Delighted she wrote

The lack of casualties in ANC operations even where bombs and explosions are used... since the emergence in the early sixties of Umkonto Wesizwe, the ANC's armed wing it has been ANC policy to avoid loss of life whenever possible. The ANC recently signed the Geneva Conventions of the 1949 and protocol 1 of 1977, concerning the protection of victims of armed conflict.

Within the space of a few hours on May 24-25, the ANC carried a series of co-ordinated guerrilla action... It is noteworthy that with one exception none of these attacks caused death, or personal injury. The exception, and it is significant—was the Ciskei ambush of the police group. The group was headed by Ciskei's Director of National Intelligence, Brigadier Charles Sebe, a carefully chosen target.[4]

One observer, however, asked, 'Are "carefully chosen targets" to be always those involving the lives of Black people?' The BBC took the cue. They noted that the ANC had up to that point committed over 37 cases fo sabotage without loss of life. It is significant to note that almost at the same time as White press was showering praises on the ANC for its non-violence, ANC guerrillas had killed black people in Vendaland. The BBC was commited to the non-violent view of the ANC. When a white police station at Booysen was attacked in 1980 and the ANC claimed the operation as its own the BBC immediately concluded that the operation had been carried out by the Azanian Peoples Liberation Army (APLA), the military wing of the Pan Africanist Congress.

The white settlers continue with violence

In December 1981, a patriotic Azanian lawyer, Griffith Mxenge was found beheaded in Durban. This babaric act pointed at the racist government of Pieter Botha. That same year activists of the ANC who were involved in the sabotage of the Sasol (oil) plant in 1980 were sentenced to death. Many African revolutionaries and patriots began to ask, 'How long will the ANC leaders and their white liberal friends continue to be more concerned about the lives of the Europeans than about the lives of the African oppressed people? How long will the blowing up of electric pylons, buildings and such other things, be equivalent to African lives. Is African life as cheap as that of a chicken?'

In 1981 and again in 1982 Oliver Tambo, President of the ANC, said his organization would confront the Boers 'face to face'. But there is no evidence that these sentiments have been translated into action. Non-violence is entrenched in the Communist Party of South Africa, which in turn controls the ANC.

A prominent leader of the South African Communist Party who has been hailed as a 'hero' by the ANC, Abraham Fischer, gave his reasons for joining the 'Communist' Party of South Africa. He said,

> I believed when I joined the Communist Party of South Africa that South Africa has set out on a course which could lead only to civil war of the most vicious kind... Algeria provided a perfect historical example of that. I believed moreover and still believe that such a civil war can never be won by the whites of this country. They might win some initial rounds. In the long run the balance of forces is against them, both inside and

outside the country... But win or lose, the consequences of civil war would be horrifying and permanent.

Clearly, it is imperative that an *alternative solution* be found, for *in truth civil war is no solution.*

In reply to Abraham Fischer's statement *Azania Contact* commented, 'After substituting ''my kith and kin'' for ''Whites of this country'' and ''armed struggle'' for ''civil'' war, one is left with no doubt as to the aims of the South African Communist Party in infiltrating the liberation movement in South Africa.'[5] Addressing a Steve Biko commemoration, Duizer Mqhaba of the Azanian Peoples Organization said, 'Whites befriend us for their benefit and whatever they do for blacks should be treated with caution and suspicion.' Referring to Joe Slovo who was then in charge of Umkonto Wesizwe, the ANC military wing, Mqhaba charged, 'If Slovo is recognised as a freedom fighter, then I might as well resign from the struggle.'[6]

In reply to the discontented Azanians, Mr Tambo confessed that his ANC had thus far conducted the struggle with 'immense restraint because we have bound ourselves by a morality which is not understood by even many of our people.'[7]

The policy of non-violence and 'moderation' did of course, give the ANC a considerable amount of 'respectability' particularly among those who did not want to countenance the fact that Azanians are a dispossessed people and have an inalienable right to self-determination. In Western countries such as Britain where the Anti-Apartheid Movement has its headquarters, ANC was given tremendous publicity and finance and treated as if it were the only liberation movement in South Africa. It was probably through the influence of its white admirers that Chief Luthuli the ANC President was given the 1961 Nobel Peace Prize for persistently pursuing the policy of non-violence.

In 1961, writes Brian Bunting:

> Over 1000 delegates attended the All African People's Conference held in Pietermaritzburg on 25 and 26 March and heard an inspiring address by Nelson Mandela, whose ban from attending gatherings had only recently expired. The conference called for a *national convention* of elected representatives of all adult men and women, without regard to race, creed or colour, to be held not later than May—the day on which the new Republic was to be proclaimed—to draw a constitution for South Africa. If the government ignored this demand, the

people would be called upon to organize mass demonstrations on the eve of the declaration of the Republic...

This call for national convention was a reasonable, democratic demand which found support among wide sections of the people White and non-White.[8]

Of course, this was not the first time that African leaders had called for a national convention to draft a democratic constitution that would solve South Africa's problems. These demands had always been rejected with contempt, and this was no exception. As Brian Bunting writes,

But the government's reaction to it (national convention) was typically intransigent. A special General Law Amendment Act was propelled through the 1961 session of Parliament empowering an Attorney-General; if he considered it necessary in the interests of public safety or the maintenance of public order, to direct that an arrested person be detained in jail for up to twelve days without bail.

Homes and offices were raided by the Special Branch of the police, and all the leaders who could be found were held under the twelve-day no bail law... During the last ten days of May all police leave was cancelled and army units were brought to a state of emergency for service![9]

This was a clear indication that 'moderation' and non-violence had failed. For instance, Umkhonto Wesizwe, the sabotage wing of the ANC carried out 193 acts of sabotage between 1961 and 1964. Commenting on the ANC sabotage attempts, Edward Feit says,

Althouth the organization of the underground ANC and Umkonto represented considerable achievement under extreme pressure from a vigilant Government, its actual effects were considerably less than its leaders had hoped. The individual acts of sabotage with few exceptions were minor and did insignificant damage. The average monthly value of the damage done was about £90.00 sterling and for the Eastern Cape it was about £5,800 in all. If the reported and unreported values of sabotage for the country as a whole are computed, they come to little more than £62,000 at the outside. This is hardly enough to damage and shake a modern industrial economy, particularly one whose budget runs to some £50,000,000. In other words, for all the courage and resourcefulness of the men who undertook sabotage, the damage they did had little more than a nuisance value. It was certainly not on a scale either to shake the South African Government or frighten the Whites into surrendering their privileged position.[10]

ANC gives up moderation

In 1967 South Africa reacted to the 'terrorists' by quickly introducing the Terrorism Act. The terrorists were no longer just PAC/POQO militants. The traditionally moderate ANC had joined in violent action as they saw no other viable course of action. For while they had maintained their tactics of moderation and non-violence, their people had been killed. To act was only to acknowledge reality.

In August 1965, the editor of *Africa and the World*, Douglas Rodgers observed,

> Most of the grounds for difference between the PAC and the ANC have now disappeared because the pressure of events has driven the ANC in all essential practical respects to accept the position taken by the PAC. All that really remains so far as the immediate situation is concerned is organizational rivalry.

Yet this rivalry is so intense that the ANC, unless it wishes to deliver some particular broadside attack, will not recognize the existence of the PAC let alone give credit to any of its members. [11]

In August 1967 the ANC guerrillas were reported fighting Smith's troops in Rhodesia side by side with ZAPU. In a communique issued on 19 August, James Chikerema, Vice President of the Zimbabwe African People's Union (ZAPU) and Oliver Tambo Preident of the ANC said that they had formed an alliance and were fighting in Rhodesia. 'We wish to declare here,' they announced, 'that the fighting that is going on in Wankie area is indeed being carried out by a combined force of ZAPU and ANC which marched into the country as comrades-in-arms'. Politically, many people felt that an effective alliance would have been that between the ANC and the PAC on one hand and that of ZAPU and ZANU on the other. After all this was what the OAU had been working for. But ZAPU did not recognize ZANU and the ANC refused to have anything to do with PAC.

Commenting on the ANC battles in Rhodesia, *The Nationalist* (organ of TANU) in Dar Es Salaam said: 'Freedom fighters must... study and know the tactics of the enemy to impose its type of war on the freedom fighters... For instance,' the paper continued,

> let me go back to the Wankie affair. The concentration of forces in the Wankie area was basically wrong from the guerrilla point of view. The concentration of forces in one area had a uniting effect on the enemy instead of dividing and splitting the enemy, Vorster came to the aid of Smith because ANC fighters were in Rhodesia so the story goes.
>
> Smith, Vorster and Salazar should never be given a chance like this to help each other. This can be done by intensifying guerrilla warfare in South Africa, Rhodesia and Portuguese Angola and Mozambique simultaneously.

Despite the criticism that was levelled against the ANC on its methods of guerrilla warfare and its 'ZAPU—ANC Alliance'—the important thing to note is that ANC did find itself forced by circumstances to revise its policy of non-violence. It gave up hope that there could ever be any useful 'dialogue'.

References:
1. *The Journal of Modern African Studies*, Volume 8, Number 1, 1970.
2. *Ibid.*
3. Mandela's Statement from the dock in Pretoria Supreme Court, 20 April 1964, at the opening of the defence.
4. *New African*, IC Magazines Ltd London, July 1981.
5. *Azania Combat*, London, October 1980.
6. *Sowetan*, Johannesburg, 14 September 1982.
7. *The Times*, London, December 1982.
8. Brian Bunting, *The Rise of the South African Reich* (Revised Edition), p.213.
9. *Ibid.*
10. *The Journal of Modern African Studies*, Vol.8, No. 1, 1970.
11. *Africa and the World*, August 1965, p.12.

15. Bantustans—A Plot Against Africans

The history of South Africa shows that the landing of Jan van Riebeeck on the southern tip of Africa led to the extermination of the Khoisan people: the robbing of Africans of their land in the Cape colony and the overthrow of African governments. In 1835 Jan van Riebeeck's descendants, the Boer treekers left the Cape colony to start a process of national dispossession of all the indigenous people of Azania. Piet Retief the Boer leader, later killed by King Dingane, spoke of the determination of his people to preserve proper relations between master and servant.

Today the racist policy of the Bantustans involves not only white supremacy, political oppression and economic exploitation of the indigenous African people, but the land question is central. The total population of South Africa is 30,000,000 people. Of these four million are white settlers, three per cent of the population are Indians while the vast majority of the population are indigenous Africans. The settlers have allocated to themselves 87% of the total land area, while 25,000,000 Africans are expected to occupy the 'homelands' or Bantustans, the remaining 13% of land. As one writer has observed:

> The white farmers in South Africa occupy 92.2 million hectares which amounts to 75% of the total land surface of the country. Of these white owned farms 106,001 live off the exploitation of cheap black labour. 68.5% of these farms are bigger than 80 hectares and 23.9% are over 860 hectares.
>
> The Bantustans or 'reserves' of the Transkei created by the South African fascists in accordance with their policy of separate development, harbour 41% of the African population and comprises only 13.5 million hectares. A commission set up by the South African fascist authorities pointed out that 30% of the total land area of the Transkei was completely eroded and therefore unporductive; 40% of the land area was semi-eroded

which left only 30% arable land! Thus African reserves, in which the people were unable to seek out a living, were calculatingly designed to act as a reservoir of cheap native labour.[1]

The bad relations between the indigenous Africans and the Boers stemmed in part from the trekker Nazi like philosophy. These Nazi attitudes have persisted and were clearly revealed during the Second World War (1939-1945). To sabotage the war effort Hertzog the Prime Minister of South Africa, said,

> Only when the war operations are properly considered will it be realized how hopeless the war already is lost, and how necessary it is for South Africa to withdraw immediately from it. Nothing but that can save our country from disaster. On land the superiority of Germany is beyond argument and in the air she has shown daily that she is England's superior.

A Defence Minister in Hertzog's cabinet, Oswald Pirow shared his Prime Minister's Nazi sympathies. In 1939, Pirow visited Hitler, Salazar and Franco. Pirow wanted former German colonies like South West Africa and Tanganyika handed over to Hitler and his views were warmly received. A German Consul at the time in Capetown went as far as to say that 'if the Union of South Africa had more men like Pirow, we'd be back in Africa in no time at all.' This was a response to Pirow's statement that: 'I shall look forward with pleasure to the return of the German to Africa, since the Nazis are the only people who know how to treat the natives.'

To a British journalist's question on whether the return of the Nazis to Africa would not be dangerous, Pirow replied,

> No, the Nazis would be a great help to us. There are too many people in the Union of South Africa who harbour silly ideas about the 'rightful freedom' of the natives. In the opinion of the majority the day the Bantu (African) gains his freedoms will mark the end of white civilisation on the African continent. The colour bar and all that it implies must be upheld at all costs. The Nazis, I know would assist us.

Asked if he believed in democracy, Pirow answered:

> I do not believe that irresponsible people should be permitted to endanger the national interests of South Africa. I am referring

particularly to individuals who would abolish much of our native legislation, who would damage our relations with certain foreign states, and who would have South Africa involved in the war.

In his *Mein Kampf*, Adolf Hitler wrote:

It was the Aryan alone who founded a superior type of humanity; therefore he represents the archtype of what we understand by the term: MAN... It was not only mere chance that the first forms of civilization arose where the Aryan came into contact with inferior races, subjugated them and forced them to obey his command.

These were sentiments which the Boer leadership always held. Daniel F. Malan, the man who first coined the word 'apartheid' and through whom the present Nationalist Party came into power, expressed similar views when he declared:

This history of the Afrikaners reveals a determination and a definiteness of purpose which makes one feel that Afrikanerdom is not the work of man but a creation of God. We have a divine right to be Afrikaners. Our history is the highest work of art of the Architect of the centuries.

Verwoerd advocated support for the Nazis and their policies through his newspaper, *Die Transvaler*. For instance, in 1954 when he saw the progress the African people of Azania were making in the field of education, he introduced an inferior type of education called 'Bantu Education'. In support of the Bill on Bantu Education, Verwoerd said,

There is no place for him (the African) in the European community above the level of certain forms of labour. Until now, he (the African) has been subjected to a school system which drew him away from his community and misled him by showing him the green pasture of the European society in which he was not allowed to graze.

The Bantustans are a conspiracy to perpetuate the national dispossession of the African people of Azania. The champions of the Bantustans are simply trying to put into practice Hilter's ideas and Piet Retief's determination to 'preserve proper relations between master and servant'

H.R. Abercrombie, writer of *Africa's Peril* and for many years

President of the Transvaal Agricultural Union and Pretoria Chamber of Commerce, revealed the motive behind the Bantustans or so-called 'separate freedoms' when he wrote,

> Now we come to an entirely different type of individual classed collectively as the Bantu, of many tribes, but probably one common origin. Their language is full of musical charm, and lends itself to flights of oratory. It is expressive and of perfect construction. The two great branches of this family are known as Zulus or Matebele and the Basuto.
>
> The Zulus have produced some remarkable soldiers—generals with good tactical knowledge and organisers of no mean ability. In Dingaan, Chaka, Cetewayo and Lobengula they had men not afraid to challenge the white man, though with vastly different weapons. Bloodthirsty and sometimes treacherous, they have taken considerable toll of the white races of Southern Africa.
>
> The Basuto, on other hand, though a cunning fighter, as we found out in Basutoland, is not such a brave type as the Zulu. In the great chief Moshesh and Khama of Bechuanaland, they have reached their highest development. Now they are entering on their greatest struggle—the attempt to become as we are, civilised men with equal rights. We must divert them back to whence they came. Under a tribal system.[2]

As Abercrombie indicated, the Boer fear of the Africans, prompted them to find ways to divert the African development and the Bantustans were the weapon to that end. They are a convenient way of diverting and condemning the Africans to a perpetual political oppression, economic exploitation and social degradation, under Bantustan 'presidents' and 'prime ministers'manipulated by Pretoria and loyal to the racist regime. Expressing the settler fears, Abercrombie said:

> In the case where you have a small white population, such as Africa is today, a policy of equality would lead undoubtedly to intermarriage between the races. It has done so in Brazil and in Mexico and South American states. That is why the Afrikaner has rightly always set his face against social equality in every way, shape or form.[3]

The basis of the division of land into Bantustans remains unexplained, as does the reason Africans are forced to live in 'stans'.

Divide and Oppress Policy

The Bantustan policy is also an attempt to make Africans believe that they are very different. That they cannot live together peacefully even though their forefathers did centuries before Jan van Riebeeck. There was intermarriage among Africans. The rulers often contracted political marriages to promote African unity. This was still the paractice as late as 1832.

For instance, in the early thirties King Moshoeshoe I sent a head of cattle to 'buy missionaries' to preach the Gospel in Lesotho. The first and second time the cattle were captured by the Khoisan people. When for the third time the cattle were captured by the San people (Bushmen), King Moshoeshoe dicided to settle the matter by marrying two daugthers of the San chief, whose men had captured the cattle. Moshoeshoe's San wives were Rosalong and Motseola also known as Qea and Seqha.

The Boers and the English are more different than Xhosa and Zulus; the Basotho and the Bapedi and Batswana. In recent years Christianity and industrialization have increased intermarriage among various Africans. In 1970 the South African government declared Chinese in South Africa 'Whites'. One would have expected that the Bantustan purists would give the Chinese their own Chinesestan, after all the Chinese are a very different 'tribe' from the Boers.

The Bantustans are a way to ignore the numerical strength of the indigenous African people. The Boers, the English and others, and now the Chinese, are counted together. They may soon claim that their 'national unit' is the largest. Soon they will include 'Coloureds' and Indians.

In 1970 Chief Kaiser Matanzima said, 'Since self-government had been given to the Transkei seven years ago the Bantu (Africans) people have lived in traquility. I want to correct the idea that the South African government is forcing on the Bantu what they never requested.' But the reality is no African would accept 13% of the land as their own nor happily build cities as big as Johannesburg, Durban, East London, Capetown and Bloemfontein in the Bantustans. A South African research publication wrote of another chief who was offered a Bantustan in Natal.

Chief Mangosuthu Buthelezi head of the Mashongashoni Regional Authority which was set up in Mahlabathini district in 1968 expressed his attitude to the idea of 'Bantu homelands' or Bantustans in interview with DRUM in October 1968. He said that the Bantu Authorities Act was published without consent.

He and his people were therefore,under no obligation to express acceptance or objection to the proclamation of the regional authority. Chief Buthelezi pointed out however, that they had learned in 1964 that their feelings were irrelevant:*the* Government policy was compulsory not optional.[4]

Progressive and enlightened chiefs have rejected the division of their people into ethnic groupings and the balkanization of their fatherland. They know that Bantustans will perpetuate the dispossession of their people. They know that the people in the Bantustans will continue to be the reservoir of 'cheap native labour' for the mines and farms of European settlers. This is probably the reason Bantustans were never discussed with the genuine leaders of the African people.

The government justified their not consulting the Africans on its Bantustan policy when Hendrick Verwoerd said 'We also know that the great mass of the Bantu are not able to decide on a matter of this nature.'[5] De Wet Nel whom the Africans called Minister of BAD (Bantu Administration and Development) when asked if self-government of the Bantustans would be in the hands of leaders elected at the polls, replied, 'If they ask for it. *But* at this stage the present system of chiefs should be develped... If the leaders were to be elected, the people might be misled by candidates promising unattainable ideals'[6]

Political Parties Reject Bantustans

Both the Pan Africanist Congress and the African National Congress have rejected the Bantustan policy of apartheid. Expressing the views of his Party in 1961 a PAC spokesman said,

> The concept of self-government for the Bantu in their areas is a
> negation of the democratic aspirations of the African people.
> The policy of balkanization of South Africa, the encouragement
> of tribalism and the handing over of self-government to the
> Bantu when they are ready, is all an attempt to perpetuate
> white supremacy. The African people want national unity. The
> African people are struggling for a non-racial democracy in the
> whole of Africa.

An ANC spokeman expressed his suspicion about the whole thing. He said,

> I do not think the step taken by the chiefs is by any means the

right one. I suspect that the chiefs are merely trying to win back the confidence of the people. How can the Transkei be independent? ...To prove that it is not a genuine demand (for true independence), during the session of Transkeian Territorial Authority, some chiefs asked to be supplied with fire-arms to protect themselves from people who were against the Bantu Authorities.

Bantustans Need Millions of Pounds

After the Nationalist Party came into power in 1948 they appointed the Tomlinson Commission to investigate the possibility of developing the 'native reserves' as they were then called. The Tomlinson Commission under Professor F.R. Tomlinson as chairman submitted its report to the cabinet in October 1954. The Government issued its White Paper on the Report in May 1956, rejecting some of the basic recommendations of the Tomlinson Commission.

The Commission had found that one of the chief reasons African left the 'native reserves' (today's Bantustans) was the infertile land which was inadequate for their needs.

The Tomlinson Commission recommended that £25,000,000 be spent during the first five years developing the 'native reserves'.

Altogether the estimated cost of the whole programme during its first ten years amounted to £104,000,000. With this sort of beginning, the Commission anticipated that the reserve areas could be made to support a population of about seven million persons in 25 to 30 years time. It also foresaw that an additional one and one-half million persons could be housed in the reserves and supported by the earnings of migrant labourers. Still, even if its recommended rate of development was achieved, the Commission concluded that by 1981 the reserves would be able to accommodate de facto only 60% of what it estimated would then be the African population of South Africa. Thus there would still remain more Africans than whites in the so-called white areas of the country.[7]

The South African Government never followed the recommendations of its Commission. Instead of spending £25,000,000 on the reserves the government established the Bantu Investment Corporation to be capitalized initially at £500,000. Later, though they spoke of a 'sum of

£36.6 million for investment in the reserves, only £7.9 million was actually expended on the development in the five years from 1956 to 1961.'[8]

'Divine' Task of Bantustan Champions

The Bantustan champions like their Boer trekker predecessors feel they have a 'divine task'. De Wet Nel, then Minister of BAD said,

> The calling of this small White nation is to give the world the basis and the pattern on which *different races* can live in peace and safety in future, *each within its own national circle*. That is the prescription for the solution of the racial problem not only in Africa, but throughout the world... Western Civilization, and particularly Christian civilization, is one of the great powers in the world. In this southern corner of Africa we are one of the strongholds of that Western Civilization. It is our duty to see that civilization is not destroyed. Therefore, we should legislate in such a way that our civilization will be preserved.[9]

In 1963 J.H. Abraham was appointed commissioner-general to the Transkei. He is a man who believed that African nationalism was the work of 'communists' or British and American agitation. He fanatically believed that he had a 'divine task' in the Transkei Bantustan. Abraham described the Xhosa Africans as 'intellectually inferior and obsessed with sex.' Guzana said that the Xhosa people did not share Abraham's view that his was a God-given task. In August 1970, Abraham was asked to resign his post in the Transkei by Knowledge Guzana who once told Matanzima's supporters that acceptance of Bantustans was like 'using a spade to dig their own graves.'

'This is one of the biggest errors his people commit,' he said angrily,

> in thinking they are in a position of authority by divine appointment. It is not so... As regards the latest incident (in which Abraham had demanded that only Afrikaans be spoken not English), I would have spoken the language understood by the person to whom I was speaking. I would have thought this the simplest rule of courtesy... There are two official languages (in South Africa), and it is a matter of choice which language a person uses.[10]

Boundaries of the Transkei

When countries like Kenya, Zambia, Ghana, Algeria, Mozambique, Botswana and other African States became independent they claimed all their territories. This is not the case in the Bantustans of South Africa. In the Transkei for instance, there are several towns which the settler regime has not handed over to the 'free' people of this 'homeland'.

In reply to a motion by the Transkei Legislative Assembly in 1968 that the districts of Elliot, Maclear and Mount Currie, and portions of districts of Port St. Johns and Matatiele be included in the Transkei, the S.A. Government wrote to say that

> *continued representations to this effect would only tend to disturb good relations*. However *as* and *when* white-owned farms in the Umzimkhulu district were offered for sale they would be bought by the S.A. Bantu Trust. When this district was completely Trust-owned the land would be transferred to the Transkeian Government.[11]

> The land question remains unsolved in the Transkeir Bantustan. Even the 'peace' that the Pretoria propagandists claim exists as a result of classifying people according to their 'tribes' has proved unreal and temporary. The Xhosa peasants continue to fight among themselves; resulting from lack of land for cultivation and cattle-grazing. On the 16 February 1971, a Reuters reporter in Umtata wrote,

> Police yesterday counted 28 dead in bloody fights between rival tribal gangs in the remote Lusikisiki region of the Transkei.

> Twenty four men died in a full scale battle involving about 600 spear and club-wielding tribesmen on Friday night. Four more died in another battle on Sunday. Police said *the battle flared over disagreements about grazing rights*.[12]

Bantustans and Independent African States

David Dube sounded a warning to the whole of Africa in a letter to *Africa and the World* after the assassination of Tom Mboya of Kenya in 1969. The letter said:

> When Mr Tom Mboya of Kenya was assassinated, a self-confessed spy for South Africa Peter Toombs, said that the

racist regime for which he had been spying was involved. By this disbolic act the racists hoped to create instability and tribal animosity in Kenya.

South Africa was so worried by this allegation that Vorster, his chief of the secret police and his ambassador in London all felt compelled to deny the allegation. Of course, at this stage it is not known what led to the assassination of Mr Mboya. The racists may not be involved.

But independent African States must be more vigilant. The racists know that they cannot oppress the people of Azania forever. Their attempt to 'befriend' African States has not been as successful as they had hoped. All along, Vorster and his fellow racists thought that a few million Rand as 'aid' would tempt the African States to sell the dignity, freedom and independence of their people. But most African States have seen through this trick. The apartheiders are therefore, now trying to extend beyond their borders the diabolic policy of 'separate freedoms'.

This policy advocates that tribalism and racialism are a 'solution' to Africa's problems. For instance, when Nigerians or Congolese fight among themselves, it is because the apartheid solution of compartmentalising Africa into weak tribal states — called Bantustans has not been applied.

When there is a riot in Malaysia, South African racists are delighted. This proves them 'right'. People of different races cannot live together. A mistake has been made by not dividing the Malays and Chinese!

The truth of the matter is that the Boers see a threat in the unity of Africa. White supremacy can triumph only when Africa's freedom rests on tribal divisions exploited by colonial and neo-colonial forces. Where heterogeneous societies in Africa have been welded into strong nations, the racists are not happy. What would then stop them from organizing an asssassination if they believed it would disintegrate an African State and lead to tribal war and secession?...

The South African racist regime would like to see the whole of Africa void of economic power so that she can be the dumping ground for apartheid goods from South Africa preferably along tribal lines. Hence they see the balkanization of Africa acccording to tribes and races as a 'solution'[13]

South Africa a Pocket of Subversion

South Africa undertakes subversion in all Africa. When a road was built between Botswana and Zambia, South Africa became furious and questioned the existence of a boundary at Kazungula between Botswana and Zambia. South Africa hated to see Botswana becoming independent economically and identifying herself with the rest of free Africa. South Africa also tried to intervene when Botswana established diplomatic relations with Russia with subjected threats and intimidation. In recent years South Africa has pursued a policy of distabilization in Southern Africa: invasions of Angola, Mozambique, Lesotho; and threats against Botswana and Zambia. Nearly 10,000 terrorists have been armed and trained as part of a campaign to destroy Zimbabwe.

When the Prime Minister Hendrick Verwoerd was assassinated in parliament in 1966, a spokesman for the African people of Azania said:

> He was the fanatical executor of that diabolical system of exploitation and oppression that today goes by the name of apartheid—a system that has turned a whole Black population into pariahs, without home and without country in the land of their birth. The various Urban Areas Acts, the Group Areas Acts etc etc., were all designed to rob the whole Non-White population of any rights of residence in any part of the country except in the little enclave called the 'Reserves'.
>
> Dr Verwoerd did not limit himself to devising plans for the adult population, for squeezing sweated labour out of every Black man and woman in South Africa by means of the abovementioned laws, together with the Pass Laws. He also masterminded the Bantu Education Act for the stultification of the young mind as well as sealing it off all contact with the stream of general culture and world civilization.
>
> The White herrenvolk in South Africa is mourning today for the assassination of Dr Verwoerd, Prime Minister of White South Africa. But those of us who have witnessed the dire consequences of his apartheid policy, the spiritual, moral and physical maiming of a whole people, have no more tears to shed for this one man. Those of us who have witnessed the herding of human beings into black ghettoes which become the grave not only of the mortal body but of every hope and aspiration natural to man, ghettoes which breed hunger,

destitution and vice, where the plunging of a knife into a black body becomes a daily recurrence—those of us who have witnessed all this have no tears to mourn the death of this one man, the embodiment of that odious immoral perversion—racism.

We have watched the anguish of mothers who daily tread the path to the ghetto graveyards to bury their new-born babies—400 of them out of every thousand born—who know that all this appalling wastage of human life is the direct result of the vicious apartheid policy, cannot stay to mourn the death of this one man. We who have lived under a system of perpetual violence every moment of the day and night cannot be surprised when this same violence spills over on its perpetrators.[14]

South Africa plans to create several Bantustans: four are already 'independent'. Fortunately through the pressure of the Organization of African Unity and the United Nations—no state in the world has as yet recognized these settler-created states.

References:
1. *Azania News*, March 1970.
2. H.R. Abercrombie, *Africa's Peril*, p.45.
3. *Ibid*.
4. *Drum*, October 1968.
5. Gwendolen M. Carter, Thomas Karis, Newell M. Stultz, *South Africa's Transkei*, p.65.
6. *Our Africa*, June 1961.
7. Gwendolen M. Carter, Thomas Karis, Newell M. Stultz, *South Africa's Transkei*, pp.43-44.
8. *Ibid*, p.45.
9. *Ibid*, p.61.
10. *Sunday Tribune*, August 16 1970.
11. *Zambia Daily Mail*, 2 December 1970.
12. *A Survey of Race Relations 1969*, pp.127-128.
13. *Africa and the World*, August 1969.
14. Unity Movement of South Africa press statement, Lusaka, 7th September, 1966.

16. The Struggle Continues

From 1965 to 1969, the South African Government claimed that it had crushed POQO (PAC) and other subversive organizations. In 1970, for the first time the Government admitted that the 1963 POQO Uprising led by PAC would have killed 1,000 whites if the police had not used their newly acquired powers. General Van der Bergh said that neither martial law nor a state of emergency could have coped up with the PAC.

The regime stepped up its propaganda work through its Radio South Africa and other media. Kaiser Matanzima and other Bantustan leaders were projected as spokesmen for the dispossessed Azanian people. The Bantustan leaders promised to fight 'terrorists' side by side with the white settlers. Some of these Bantustan chiefs even collected monies from the poor Africans—living in their areas as contributions to the 'anti-terrorist fund'.

With the Pan Africanist Congress and the African National Congress banned the African voice was weak. But students who were members of the Pan Africanist Congress continued to educate and mobilize other students on national questions. This mobilization was carried out under extreme police intimidation and harrassment. The liberal English NUSAS (National Union of South African Students), being a white organization with some Black university students participation was not banned, and played a role in exposing the oppression of the Black people of Azania. Unfortunately, NUSAS had always been sympathetic to the liberal Congress Alliance led by the Communist Party of South Africa and could not act as the advocates for the Blacks.

In 1970, dissatisfied with the NUSAS and its allies, the black students formed their own organization, the SASO (South African Students Organization). The Black students had experienced what Mangaliso Robert Sobukwe, President of the Pan Africanist Congress had said at the inaugural conference of his party in December 1959.

The PAC leader had said,

> We have admitted that there are Europeans who are intellectual
> converts to the African's cause, but because they benefit
> materially from the present set-up, they cannot completely iden-
> tify themselves with that cause.
>
> Thus it is, as South Africa's history so ably illustrates, that
> whenever Europeans 'co-operate' with African movements, they
> keep on demanding checks and counter-checks, guarantees and
> the like, with the result that they stultify and retard the move-
> ment of the Africans.

SASO had learnt this from bitter experience. When the black students
left NUSAS to form SASO, they said, 'Black students owe their first
allegiance to the black community with whom they share burden and
injustices of apartheid'.

When SASO was founded it was attacked; called 'racialist' and
criticized for not co-operating with the 'multi-racial' NUSAS. The South
African Indian Congress, which took part in the Kliptown charter of the
Congress Alliance in 1955, accused SASO of advocating the same policies
that had been pursued by the Pan Africianist Congress before it was
banned.

Undaunted the SASO embarked on the mobilization of all sectors
of the Black community. They rejected the Bantustan tribal chiefs and
described 'gains' of the Bantustan policy as gimmicks calculated to buy
more time for the South African Government which was being over-
taken by events in neighbouring countries. SASO also initiated self-help
projects such as clinics, literacy classes and the like for the Black community. Despite government bans on its leaders, the SASO rapidly gained
wide acceptance among the black people and gave them renewed hope
after the PAC and ANC were forced underground.

SASO was a student body. When students left school there was no
political party for them to join. Indeed, the whole Black Consciousness
movement which had developed needed a political home. On the 24 April
1971, a conference was held in Bloemfontein which had as its main theme
the co-operation and co-ordination of the efforts of all black organizations which have an identical national outlook. At this conference, SASO
(South African Students Organisation), IDAMASA (Inter-denominational
African Ministers' Association of South Africa), IACA (African Independent Churches Association), ASSECA (Association for the Education
and Cultural Advancement of African People of South Africa) and

YWCA (Young Women's Christian Association) were represented.

The Bloemfontein Conference elected an Ad Hoc Committee. Its task was to invite more black people and organizations to a large conference. In August 1971, this culminated in the Pietermaritzburg conference; its theme the 'Development of the African Community'. Over 100 representatives from educational, sporting, welfare, religious and students' organizations attended. Among the speakers who addressed the conference were Drake Koka, Steve Biko, Mrs E. Kuzwayo and Mrs Mabiletsa.

The following resolutions were adopted:

a. That all African organizations be asked to join in the formation of a confederate organization.
b. That these organizations should work with other black organizations toward the realization of the black man's aspirations.
c. That a national political organization be formed and operate outside the apartheid Government system and policy.
d. That such a national organization must devote itself to representing African opinion on a political basis and to promoting community development programmes on education, economic and cultural aspects.

On the 14 January 1972, the Black Peoples Convention Ad Hoc Committee announced the formation of a black peoples political party under the banner of Black Consciousness. In its statement, the BPC (Black Peoples Convention) Ad Hoc Committee declared that,

it is the inalienable birthright of any community to have a political voice to articulate and realise the aspirations of its members.

In this our country, Africans, Coloured and Indians comprise the Black Community which has been deprived of this inalienable right; and for too long there has been a political racialism in the black community.

The Ad Hoc Committee is therefore working towards the formation of a Black Peoples' Political Movement whose primary aim is to unite and solidify black people with a view to liberating and emancipating them from both psychological and physical oppression.

Our interests therefore, lie within the black community and our sole aim will be directed towards realising its needs, which needs will coincide with those of all Black people throughout the world.

It is therefore, essential and imperative that all black people, individuals and organizations, should pool their resources together in order to achieve their aspirations. Their future destiny and ultimate happiness is in their hands.

The Black Consciousness movement moved quickly. On 8-10 July, 1972, the Black Peoples Convention held its Pietermaritzburg conference. It was well attended. The constitution was adopted and the organization formally launched. At the conference's conclusion an interim executive was elected:

Mr A. Mayatula: President
Mr M. Shezi: Vice President
Mr D.K. Koka: Secretary-General
Mr S. Cooper: Public Relations Officer
Mr A. Dlamini: National Organizer

The Black Peoples' Convention resolved:

To operate openly as an overt peoples movement.
To establish branches throughout the country.
To work on membership drive towards a target of 1,000,000 in three years.

After the conference spontaneous action occurred. There were bus strikes in Johannesburg and Durban. There was a widely publicized dock workers' strike in Durban, which caught the attention of the entire world press. Exiled leaders of the African National Congress of South Africa, attached to the long ineffective South African Congress of Trade Unions (SACTU), claimed they initiated these strikes, but it was the Black Consciousness movement which was responsible.

When the Durban City Council banned buses in Chartsworth as a result of the bus strike by th Black workers, the BPC issued a statement which read:

It is important to remember at a time like this that these acts of racism against us are not isolated. These are part of a master plan by the whiteman to keep us in perpetual servitude and to seal the shackles that bind us in bondage. It was only a while ago that our brothers and sisters in Gelvandale, Port Elizabeth were affected similarly by transport hurdles imposed by the white man. The people of Gelvandale preferred to walk to Port Elizabeth and back rather than sell their souls to the cut-throat price of the white man. Let us remember that the government is not out to please us all. The government is out on a deliberate campaign to destroy us physically and spiritually.

Mtuli Shezi, Vice President of the interim executive committee of the Black Peoples' Convention died. Before Mr Shezi died, he related events leading to the 'accident' which caused his death.

He said he had originally quarrelled with some white employees in the South African Railways. He had objected to the bad treatment these white employees had meted out to black women at a railway station some days before the 'accident'. What was the accident?

Some days after his quarrel with the white Railway employees, Shezi went through Germiston. It was on the 12 December 1972. he was apparently spotted by one of the European Railway employees with whom he had quarrelled. This white man chased Mr Shezi, caught and overpowered him. He then pushed him onto the rails in front of an on-coming train. After being knocked down and dragged by the train, Mr Shezi sustained a number of injuries. These injuries included a fractured pelvis, a dislocated hip and a raptured bladder. Five days after being taken to the hospital Mr Shezi died. The police said they suspected no foul play!

The Black Peoples Convention was not intimidated. The organization held its first conference on 16-17 December 1972 and elected as President Mrs Winnifred Kgware, a 54-year old teacher and mother of four. 'You have opened a new chapter in the book of Black development in South Africa,' Mrs Kgware said addressing the inaugural congress of the BPC. 'We have embarked on something that Africa has long been waiting for,' she concluded.

Until then some people were still not convinced that the Black Consciousness movement was a genuine liberation movement. But one of the highlights was invitation to this historic congress of Ntsu Mokhehle, President of the Basutoland Congress Party. Mr Mokhehle officially opened the congress in absentia. He was a prohibited immigrant to South Africa.

Mokhehle had long been involved in the African Revolution. He attended the All Africa Peoples Conference called by Dr Kwame Nkrumah in Accra in 1958 which accelerated the movement of liberation. He was also a member of the steering committee. When the leaders of the Black Peoples Convention invited him, he spoke to the conference by means of a tape-recorded speech. The delegates to the conference listened attentatively.

For ten years since Sharpeville in 1960, the African people could not organise openly. The BPC now organised openly. This does not mean that it was easy. The leaders of the Black Consciousness movement were subjected to bannings, restrictions, imprisonment and passport refusal to travel abroad; like when Mr Nyameko Barney Pityana, Secretary-General of SASO was refused a passport to tour the USA at the invitation of the Department of State's Education Travel Programme. The SASO T-shirt was also banned. The re-designing of the shirt did not help. But the Black Consciousness movement became more militant.

In a dramatic move at their Hammernskraal Conference, SASO expelled its President Temba Sono. Sono had argued that SASO had to learn to be flexible in its approach and to 'talk to our enemies'. He called for open-mindedness towards the leaders of the Bantustans, white liberals even to the security police. Mr Ben Khoapa, Director of Black Community Programmes summed up the students' mood:

> Black students are increasingly resisting efforts to get them to co-operate in their own educational genocide. No longer can they be contained by white rhetoric; nor can they be seduced into rejecting the interests of their own people. They have learnt what a large number of black people are beginning to learn from our young people that the revolution is not over and it is not just beginning, it's continually with us.

The militancy of the Black consciousness movement spread to the church. *Eassys on Black Theology* edited by Mokgethi Motlhabi were published by the Black Theology project of the University Christian Movement and Black Viewpoint published by th Black Community Programmes. *Essays on Black Theology* was banned on 28 July, 1972.

In 1972 relations between the Black Consciousness movement and the Natal Indian Congress were still not good. The militancy of the Black organizations was said to be hindering co-operation with the Natal Indian Congress. But the 1973 Secretariat report of the Natal Indian Congress said, 'In pursuit of its stated policy of working with organizations sharing its goals, the NIC has *attempted* to work with both BPC and SASO.' In fact, Mr G. Serwspersodh chairman of the Natal Indian Congress was one of the many speakers at the Sharpeville Commemmoration on the 21 March 1973, organized by the Black Peoples Convention.

The Frelimo Rally

In September 1974, the Black Consciousness movement organized a rally to express solidarity with Frelimo, who had just defeated the Portuguese colonial government in a guerrilla war. The Black Peoples' Convention and SASO jointly announced plans to hold a rally in Durban, Capetown, Port Elizabeth and Johannesburg to coincide with the independence of Mazambique under Frelimo. In public places such as clinics, schools and halls were painted with slogans like 'Viva Frelimo', 'Viva Sobukwe', 'Viva Azania'. They were painted at night.

According to the *Sunday Times* 22 September 1974, a SASO representative had already approached a Frelimo leader in Lourenco Marques (now Maputo). Three speakers were expected to address the rally. But the South African Government banned the meeting, and arrested several of the Black Consciousness movement leaders charging them under the Terrorism Act. Reporting the events of 25 September 1974 a SASO pamphlet entitled *The Frelimo Rally—The Facts and Evaluation* says:

> On Wednesday, 25th September 1974, at about 17.30, over 2,000 people gathered outside the Curries Fountain on the embankment opposite the entrance to the stadium, despite the banning of the Rally. The atmosphere was thick with expectation. The hum of excitement and genuine solidarity were indicative of the Black Community's mood.
>
> White police of course, were already present, having cordoned off the area around Gurries Fountain and preventing anyone from entering the stadium. Reinforcements continued to arrive with all their paraphernelia — dogs, swagger-sticks, riot vans—a pathetic show of force.
>
> By 17.40 the number of people had increased to between 4,000 and 5,000. Encouraged by the free wheeling atmosphere and unconcerned by the racist show of force, the crowd began to sing and dance. The national anthem, 'Nkosi Sikelel iAfrika,' was chanted, the Black power salute was given, and many people shouted slogans including 'Viva Frelimo'.
>
> The police, however, without warning unleashed the already excited Alsatian dogs into the peaceful and unarmed crowd. Screams filled the air as women and men were bitten by dogs. One of the people bitten by these savage dogs was a pregnant woman.

Some of those later charged under the Terrorism Act for the Frelimo rally were:

- Gilbert Kaborone 'Kaunda' Sedibe, President of the University of North Students' Representative Council
- Abosolom Zithulele Cindi, Secretary-General of the BPC at the time of arrest
- Sodeque Variova, SASO member and leader of the Peoples' Experimental Theatre and SASO.
- Strivivase Rajoo Moodley, former SASO Publications Director and Editor of the SASO newsletter.
- Rubin Hore, Vice-President of SASO when arrested.
- Sathasivan 'Saths' Cooper, former Public Relations Officer of the Black Peoples' Convention.
- Justice Edmund Lindane Muntu Myeza, former President of SASO and Secretary-General of SASO at the time of detention.
- Mosiuoa Gerlad Patric Lekota, permanent Organizer of SASO since 1973.
- Maitshwe Nchaupe Aubrey Mokoape, Founder member of BPC and SASO.
- Nkwenkwe Vincent Nkomo, National Organizer of BPC when arrested.
- Pondelani Jeremiah Mefolovhedwe, national President of SASO and final year B.Sc. student of the University of the North at the time of his arrest.

The charge sheet numbering 104 pages alleged that the accused had during the period between 1968 and October 1974, conspired with one another to:

> Transform the state by unconstitutional revolutionary and/or violent means.
>
> Condition the African, Indian and Coloured population groups of the Republic of South Africa for violent revolution.
>
> Create and forster feelings of racial hatred, hostility and antipathy by Blacks towards whites and/or the state. Denigrate whites and represent them as inhuman oppressors of Blacks, and to induce, persuade and pressurize Blacks to totally reject the white man and his way of life, and to defy him.
>
> Make, produce, publish or distribute subversive and anti-

white utterances, writings, poems, plays and/or drama.

Discourage, hamper, deter or prevent foreign investments in the conomy of the Republic, and to call upon foreign investors to disengage themselves from the South Africa economy, or sections of the said economy.

Black Reactions to Persecution

The spokesmen for the Black Consciousness movement said, 'So long as our dignity is trodden upon, so long as we are subjected to humiliation, there can be no trust nor peace between us and the oppressor.' Another spokesman of the Black people said that the South African Government was using the Frelimo Rally as an excuse to 'crush SASO, BPC, BAWU and other Black Consciousness organizations. By bleeding our organizations of effective leadership they assume the Black movement will die a natural death.'

The Black Consciousness movement was undeterred. Expressions of support poured in as Black people throughout the country visited the offices of BPC and SASO 'to keep the fires burning'.

The Death of Tiro: His Spirit Lives on

Onkgopotse Ramothibi Abraham Tiro was killed by a parcel bomb in Botswana where he had sought asylum. He was one of the five members of the Black Consciousness movement who left the country in 1973. Tiro was the President of the South African Students' Movement (SASM). The Botswana Government proclaimed his death as a result of his activities on behalf the rights of the Africans.

Their statement went on to observe that

Onkgopotse Tiro had incurred the displeasure of certain powerful circles in South Africa. Mr Tiro's sudden and cruel death will in no way detract from the *validity of his criticism of education in South Africa*. The Botswana Government wishes to state unequivocally that this kind of terrorism will not make it change its attitude towards those who seek refuge in Botswana from the oppression of their own countries.

Mr Tiro's sudden and *cruel death will in no way detract from the validity of his criticism of education in South Africa*, prophecized a Botswana Government official. On 16 June 1976, Soweto school children confronted the police shouting: 'We are not Boers.' 'Afrikaans is the oppressors' language.' 'We want our land.' 'Viva Azania.' Generated by the Black Consciousness movement, the Azanian struggle for freedom intensified. 'South Africa Explodes' shout the headlines of most newspapers.

Over 1000 children were mercilesly massacred by the South African regime. Many more were wounded. Hundreds were thrown into jails. Thousands fled from South Africa. Dozens of others were so remorselessly tortured they committed suicide in despair.

The Soweto Uprising Was Extraordinary

The Soweto uprising was extraordinary. It was led by children inspired by the ideas of the Black Consciousness movement. In its opinion column one newspaper commented,

> At Sharpeville 16 years ago and Carltonville in 1973, it was the anger of adults that burst out at the bestial humiliation... in their own country. But today at Soweto it is the voice of protest from 10,000 black children against a ruthless subserviance to domination by an alien people that is setting ablaze 55 square kilometers of an apartheid settlement.
>
> The march of events registers the escalating hatred of apartheid in South Africa not just as the concern of the adults but that of infants and the totality of the country's oppressed... it is important for South African leaders of the revolution inside and outside the country to learn from the masses of Soweto, Sharpeville and other turning points that salvation of the black man lies in his total refusal to co-operate with apartheid.

For its part *Azania News* said of the childrens' revolution

> The black people of Azania are up in arms! The racist regime is in panic! The symbols of white alien domination are up in flames. The edifices of exploitation have been turned to ruins. The language of colonization has been set on the road to hell. The representatives of fascism and white racism are afraid to show their faces among the people. Three hundred and more years of sowing hatred are begetting hatred. It is not racial hatred on the part of our people... Who can oppose Azania after the people have spilled their blood for it? Who can

stubbornly refuse to acknowledge the people's love for Azania?

What is Black Consciousness?

Before SASO was banned in October 1977, it defined 'Black Consciousness' as:

   a. an attitude of mind, a way of life;
   b. its basic tenet is that the Black man must reject all value systems that seek to make him a foreigner in the country of his birth and reduce his basic human dignity;
   c. it implies awareness by the Black people of the power they wield as a group cohesion and solidarity are important facts of Black Consciousness;
   d. the Black man must build up his own value system, see himself as self-defined and not defined by others;
   e. Black Consciousness will always be enhanced by the totality of involvement of the oppressed people, hence the message of Black Consciousness has to be spread to reach all section of the Black Community;
   f. liberation of the Blackman begins first with liberation from psychological oppression of himself through an inferiority complex and second from the physical one accruing out of living in a white racist society;
   g. Black people are those who are by law or tradition, politically, socially and economically discriminated against as a group in the South African society of their aspirations.

Black Consciousness Movement, versus PAC and ANC

It was the fundamental policy of the Black Consciousness movement to co-operate with *all* Black Consciousness-oriented organizations which work outside the policy of apartheid and Bantustans, BCM declared. The Black Consciousness Movement, however, is independent of both the PAC and ANC. It has its own leader-ship and liberation programme.

However it seems that ideologically, Black Consciousness is closer to PAC. The BCM has not accepted the 'Freedom' Charter. At the fourth annual conference of SASO in Hammanskraal in July 1973, SASO's acting Permanent Organiser, Abraham Tiro urged delegates to be positive and consider the country (*Azania*) as a Black state which *belonged* only to Black people. 'This should not be construed as anti-white', he explained. 'It only means that in as much as Black people live in Europe on terms laid down by whites, whites should be subjected to the same conditions.'

The BCM also declared 21 March, Heroes' Day. Since 1961 the PAC had this date as Sharpeville Day. In 1977, nine months after the Soweto Uprising, the BCM observed 21 March as Heroes Day. They called for a week of prayer in memory of the protesters of Sharpville and a Johannesburg newspaper reported, 'Soweto mourns Sharpeville victims.'

There have also been arguments over the name *Azania* for South Africa. In September 1977 Steve Biko, the honorary President of the Black Peoples' Convention died in police custody. Over 20,000 Azanians attended his funeral. At this funeral they used AZANIA instead of the colonialist name of South Africa. Biko's coffin had his face engraved on it and a pair of broken chains with the words: 'Biko—One Azania, One Nation, One People.'

When Mangaliso Robert Sobukwe, President of the Pan Africanist Congress was laid to rest at Graaff-Reinet on the 11 March 1978, the Rand *Daily Mail* in Johannesburg reported, 'Graaff-Reinet wakes to hear of *Azania*.' The paper continued,

> The little town of Graaff-Reinet woke up with a shock at the weekend to black power salute and endless doses of freedom songs from a highly politicised black youth... The crowd stirred as the coffin was brought out of the house—the open palm salute of the PAC, carved on it... The crowd surged forward and there were intermittent shouts of *'One Azania One Nation'*. A lanky man sweating heavily shouted: 'freedom!' and the crowd roared back 'Now!'

BCM changed its name to Black Consciousness Movement of Azania in 1980. The ANC On the other hand has persistently used the name 'South Africa'. Commenting on this, *The Revolutionary Worker* said,

> Although the ANC attempted to claim the Soweto Uprising as a product of their work, it was only to cut out any real significance of it. It was also around this time that the ANC publicly began to attack the name *Azania* in a big way... was growing in popularity among the revolutionary masses... the

ANC insisted that South Africa was the only correct name for the area. Once again what this revealed was ANC's fundamental opposition to and denial of the national struggle of the Azanian people and their (ANC's) dedication to working out a compromise power-sharing agreement (with the racists).

The Revolutionary Worker continued 'Throughout 1977 Sechaba ran articles attacking the BCM as being backed by the West... Alfred Nzo, the Secretary-General of the ANC called BCM "new allies of imperialism" and "substitutes for the Bantustan leaders".' Yet it was the ANC which forged an alliance with the Bantustan leader of KwaZulu, Chief Gatsha Buthelezi, in October 1979, when they thought they could 'use' the chief and his Inkatha 'In addition to their attack on the BCM,' *The Revolutionary Worker* said,

> the ANC hit particularly hard at the leaders of the BCM, Steve Biko (before he was murdered by the South African rulers. Of course, after his death the ANC did their damnest to try and claim his mantle as their own. According to Sechaba (first quarter 1977) Steve Biko was tied in with British liberals and by implication, to U.S. imperialism.[1]

When the Black Consciousness Movement was banned in October 1977, the Azanian Peoples Organisation (AZAPO) was formed. At its congress, AZAPO, re-affirmed its total commitment to the Black-Consciousness philosophy, rejected the homelands and sad it would focus on the two cardinal issues: Black citizenship and trade unions. A white journalist Barry Streek, writing from Capetown said, 'It was on the question of workers' rights that the most marked change of emphasis from the earlier organization has taken place.'

SASO which was also banned in 1977 was replaced by the Azanian Students Organization (AZASO). Although some elements in AZASO seemed to play down black consciousness as an ideology, AZAPO as a whole was uncompromising. Speaking at the Hammanskraal symposium in May 1981, Kehla Mthembu, President of AZAPO said

> It has become rather necessary for me to reaffirm Black Consciousness, a philosophy which has been the driving force in the Black Struggle for humanity in the past two decades.
>
> Some prophets of doom have organized themselves into well-orchestrated choirs, unfortunately conducted by Black deserters and white liberals who sing a chorus that Black

Consciousness has exhausted itself or rather finished its cycle. We might suffer setbacks and go through moments of uncertainty, but we owe it to ourselves—parents, students, all black people—to emerge from this symposium more united in theory and practice... Blacks will never fully reassert their humanity before they achieve liberation.

Mthembu ended his speech saying,

I, as President of AZAPO hereby commit all revolutionary and progressive black forces to this unchallengeable and undebatable liberatory philosophy in our pursuit for a Free and liberated Azania... One Azania, One Nation, One People.

On the 2 December 1981 a headline in the Rand *Daily Mail* in Johannesburg said, 'NEWS EDITOR PLANNED TO MEET BANNED SSRC CHIEF, COURT HEARS'. The newspaper went on

Mr Thami Mazwai news editor of a black morning newspaper the *Sowetan*—detained since July—had arrangements to meet the banned Soweto Students Representative Council President, Mr Sydney Khotso Seatlholo.
   This was alleged in charges laid before a Johannesburg Regional Court Magistrate yesterday when Mr Seatlholo, 25, and Miss Mary Mmasabata Loate, 23, both of Soweto, appeared before Mr P.A.J Kotze in connection with two allegations of contravening the Terrorism Act.
   Miss Loate arranged for two South African Youth Revolutionary Council (SAYRCO) members from Botswana to contact the Azanian Peoples Organisation (AZAPO) national organizer in Soweto. Miss Loate joined the Azanian National Youth Union (AZANYU).

On the 13 January 1979, the *Natal Mercury* had carried a news story 'Plan to Bomb and Burn S.A. Building... Members of the Azanian Revolutionary Movement planned to bomb and burn Government buildings until the South African Government met their demands, a Durban Regional Court Magistrate heard yesterday.'

The two ANCs and the CPSA

In 1975 when the Black Consciousness movement was preparing for a showdown with the settlers inside South Africa, the African National Congress split into two wings—the Oliver Tambo group and Makiwane group. This split occurred when the Tambo group expelled eight of its leading members including Dr Pascal Ngakane Chief Albert Luthuli's son-in-law and Ambrose M. Makiwane.

The Makiwane group ignored the expulsion and claimed that they represented the true ANC accusing the Tambo group of having been hijacked by the white liberals in the Communist Party of South Africa. The Makiwane group said,

> The ANC of Tambo is now simply a front or cover organization used as a tool to achieve the objectivies of the SACP. Those objectives of the SACP reside in the domination of the Blacks by whites in the name of Marxism-Leninism... the Party (CPSA), not the ANC is in the vanguard role of directing the struggle for the national liberation of the African people. This accounts for the arrogance of such whites as Slovo and Carneson in giving instructions to Africans on what Africans have to do to liberate themselves. They have reduced the Tambo group of the ANC to mere puppets dancing to the music of His Master's Voice.

The Makiwane group then asked a painful question:

> For how long will White South Africans continue to dominate them (Blacks) politically and humiliate them socially? We say this practice must be stopped immediately. The Slovos and Carnesons have no right even to attend meetings of Africans where plans to overthrow white domination are discussed.*[2]

The Pan Africanist Congress has hailed the historic role the Black Consciousness Movement is playing in the liberation of Azania. PAC has not only given publicity to the activities of the BCM, but has accepted BCM as comrades-in-arms on the complete basis of equality. PAC has invited all Azanian patriotic organizations which have a contradiction with the settler racist regime to form a united patriotic front.

---

* See In Defence of the African Image and Heritage, Box 25044, Dar-Es-Salaam

The Battle for Azania and the Kliptown Charter

In 1981 and 1982 there was great pressure on the Azanians to adopt the 'Freedom' Charter and to use 'South Africa' instead of Azania. On the 14 February 1982, George Wauchope, then publicity secretary of the Azanian Peoples Organisation told the *Sunday Express* in Johannesburg that as much as he recognized the historical liberation organizations, he was aware that the Freedom Charter was also one of the catalysts that split the ANC and the PAC. He pointed out that until those organizations resolved their differences the Azanian Peoples Organization would not identify with the Freedom Charter. Wauchope drew attention to the fact that There has been a lot of puppeteering and publicity (by the settler press in South Africa) to populirise the Freedom Charter.[3] On the 3 June Khehla Mthembu President of AZAPO was interviewed on the political situation inside Azania. Among other things he replied:

> Contrary to what the media wants us to believe, Black Consciousness is growing because it is not an intellectual analysis of the black man's situation nor academical gymnastics. It is an existential experience of a people who are subjected to subjugation and exploitation...
>
> Up to 1977, white liberals had no room in the black struggle. When the clampdown became a reality, they jumped into the so-called leadership vacuum; dangling moneys and attracting the less vigilant of our people and at the same time discrediting Black Consciousness as there was no role for them to play. The white liberals were eagerly supported by their partisan media and other liberal organizations in their campaign against the Black Consciousness.[4]

Another attempt to confuse the Azanian revolutionaries came on 16 June 1982. At the commemoration meeting of the *Soweto Uprising* held at the University of Natal there was a showdown when the Azanian Students Organization (AZASO) vice-chairman, Yusuf Abba Moosa, called the meeting to pledge support for the 'Freedom' Charter.

> However, members of the Black Consciousness Movement, the Unity Movement and the Azanian People's Organization, felt this was not the proper forum for such a resolution to be raised. People, they said, had come to pay homage to the students who had died in 1976 and this should not be marred by ideological dispute.[5]

The Trade Union in the Early 1980s

When AZAPO was founded its leaders said they would address themselves to the interests of the Blacks as both a dispossessed people and economically exploited workers. In the 1960s the main trade unions were the South African Congress of Trade Unions (SACTU) and the Federation of Free African Trade Unions of South Africa (FOFATUSA). But the white settler regime's anti-labour laws were not conducive to the growth of these trade unions.

From the early 1970s onwards several trade unions were formed as labour laws for African workers were relaxed. There has been rapid growth of African trade unions subsequently, from 16,000 workers in 1969 to 59,000 in 1975, passing the 300,000 mark in 1981. In the first half of 1982 some of the large national-minded trade unions were believed to belong to five groupings:

a. The Federation of South African Trade Unions (FOSATU). It was led by Joe Foster and had a membership of over 100,000. FOSATU was itself dependent on three other large unions—the National Allied and Automobile Workers Association (NAAWU). It had over 12,000 workers and its secretary-general was Fred Sauls; Metal and Allied Workers Union (MAWU). It had 30,000 members and its secretary-general was Daivd Sibabi; National Union of Textile Workers which had a membership of 13,000 and was led by Obed Zuma.

b. The Council of Unions of South Africa (CUSA) had a membership of 50,000 and was led by Albert Mosenthal.

c. The South African Allied Workers' Union (SAAWU) had a membership of over 70,000. Its secretary-general was Sam Kikine. Thozamile Gqwetha was the President while Sisa Njikelane was organizing secretary. They were all detained during 1982.

d .The General Workers' Union (GWU) with a membership of 19,000 members was led by David Lewis.

e. The African Food and Canning Workers Union (AFCWU) had 18,500 members. Its secretary-general was Jan Theron. In 1982 40% of workers still came from Mozambique, Lesotho and Swaziland.

The trade union movement in South Africa is likely to play the most decisive role in the repossession of Azania and Azanians national and social emancipation, both as a people and as workers. The Pan Africanist Congress of Azania slogans: 'Azanian workers under settler-colonial rule, Land dispossessed and brutally exploited,' clearly put the position.

In 1982 the South African regime brutalized and harrassed trade union leaders. Mr Njikelan's house in Mdantsana was burnt, while Mr Gqweta's mother and uncle died when their house was mysteriously gutted by fire.

In August 1982, The South African Institute of Race Relations said that Mr Ernest Moabi Dipale was the 53rd person to have died in detention in recent years.

Zeph Mothopeng sentenced to 30 years imprisonment

The late 1970s were not good for the Pan Africanist Congress. A number of its guerrillas were arrested in South Africa in 1978. The Swaziland Government also adopted a hostile attitude to the PAC and a number of PAC refugees were expelled from the country. In February 1978, the President of the Pan Africanist Congress, 'Defier of the undefiable', Mangaliso Robert Sobukwe died Top officals of the Party who had been in touch with him inside Azania said he had been poisoned on Robben Island where he had been imprisoned without trial. After nine years in prison he was 'eternally' restricted to the town of Kimberly until he died. Johannes B. Vorster's regime had vowed that Sobukwe would never be released from jail or detention 'this side of eternity'.

To compound matters David Sibeko, PAC's ablest foreign affairs secretary was assassinated in Dar-Es-Salaam by Boss elements infiltrated into PAC There was confusion within PAC. Boss seemed to be gaining the upper hand and succeeding in destroying the PAC. At the same time Potlako K. Leballo was asked to step down from the leadership of the Pan Africanist Congress. He was said to be sick and unable to lead the Party. But it would seem there was dissatisfaction with his leadership. He had become a liability to the PAC.

Inside Azania, Zeph Mothopeng the veteran leader was arrested with 17 others. He was charged under the Terrrorism Act and in 1979 sentenced to 30 years imprisonment on Robben Island. Reporting on the famous 'Bethal Trial of 18', the *Sunday Times* (Johannesburg) of 1 July 1979, said:

South Africa's biggest terror trial, and one of the longest in the

country's judicial history wound up this week when the Pan
Africanist Congress supporters were jailed for underground
activities.

They were sentenced to a total of 162 years imprisonment... The statistics of the trial have set their own records... it
has taken 165 court sitting days, 5,200 pages of evidence and
argument were recorded, and 86 co-conspirators were involved... Almost the entire trial including the marathon 21-hour
judgment was held in camera.

Mothopeng, one observer said will go down in the history of Azania
as the leader who orchestrated the Soweto Uprising in 1976. His close
colleagues called him 'lion'. Mothopeng was brave but very modest.

Writing about him one journalist said that he and his PAC comrades
inside Azania were determined that the cause of black nationalism would
not be stifled, after PAC was banned. Zeph Mothopeng operated quiet-
ly from his private quarters in Soweto, right under the noses of the security police. He gathered groups of youths around him, injecting them with
the spirit of black nationalism and Pan Africanism.

The cells he was able to form multiplied rapidly. The underground
movement grew in scope and depth and converged with the patriotic efforts of Steve Biko, who was later to die after receiving injuries while
in the custody of South African secret police.

Paradoxically, it was the white judge, Justice Curlewis, at
Mothopeng's trial who unwittingly provided an epitaph which will un-
doubtedly be quoted by Azanians long after Uncle Zeph's death when
he said, Mothopeng had 'acted to sow seeds of anarchy and revolution.
The riots he had engineered and predicted had eventually taken place
in Soweto on 16 June 1976, and Kagiso the next day'[6]

Pokela becomes PAC Chairman

In February 1981 after serving 13 years imprisonment on Robben Island
and escaping from South Africa, John Nyati Polela arrived abroad in
Tanzania. He was unanimously elected Chairman (President) of the Pan
Africanist Congress. In January 1982, Chairman Nyati Pokela addressed the 38th Ordinary Session of the OAU Liberation Committee held
in Kinshasa. It was his first appearance before this august body. He said,

Another factor which puzzled me... is the superficial approach
and tendency to make belief that with bombings of certain

installations inside the country the Azanian revolution has suddenly begun and is about to be completed in the near future.

This is an exercise in self-deception. It is however, true that the struggle of our people is gaining momentum daily, but the armed struggle was started by the PAC and it is a long and ardous one... and all the forces opposed to the regime must be galvanised for the revolution. No single force can successfully carry the Azanian revolution to the total exclusion of other patriotic forces. This is an objective reality.

Moreover, Comrade Chairman, the South African racist regime cannot be brought down by merely attacking—no matter how frequently—installations and other inanimate objects. The regime is maintained in power by the army and the police. It is these two pillars of apartheid state that have to be vigorously and systematically attacked if the regime is to be brought down. To radically change the minds of the settler racists and their supporters the armed struggle must be primarily at the level of mortals.

Chairman Pokela reminded all PAC members and the Azanian people that 'Ours is a peoples' war that involves every mother's child. It is the struggle of the people. Therefore everybody who has a contradiction with the enemy must be involved.'

After Pokela assumed the leadership of the PAC, a 'Conference on Terrorism' was organized by the Centre for International Politics at the University of Potchefstroom. Significantly, it was addressed by the South African Chief of Security and Police, Major-General Johan Coetzee and General Constad Viljoen of the Defence Force who told the Conference, 'The outlawed Pan Africanist Congress is undergoing a process of renewal.' He also spoke of PAC being 'attracted to the country-side terrorist actions.'

In 1982 writing about the PAC and the ANC, the author of *South African Capitalism and Political Opposition* said,

The PAC has maintained a popular following inside South Africa... In general, sympathetic critics of the ANC have frequently levelled three charges against the External Mission: (1) Solidarity work and international diplomacy have absorbed the exile leadership to the point, where internal work has been neglected; (2) the continued emphasis on sabotage activities have all too often aimed at 'spectacular success' rather than as a means of politically mobilizing the oppressed; and (3) the combination of aging leadership and over ten years of exile has rendered the ANC increasingly out-of-touch with changing moods and new political developments within South Africa.[7]

Whatever mistakes the Pan Africanist Congress may have made, there is no countering the fact that their political line is correct and supported by the majority of Azanians. One of the most celebrated speeches of the PAC Chairman both inside and outside Azania was that delivered to the United Nations General Assembly on 9 November 1982.

He correctly summed up the story of a dispossessed people when he said,

> Our country AZANIA was first colonised in 1652 when the Dutch East India Company decided to establish a half-way house... Moreover, Mr Chairman, it was the treacherous South Africa Act of 1909 passed by the British Parliament, the supposed symbol of democracy, that our country, Azania was given the appelation Union of South Africa. The Union here referring to the union between the two white communities against the African majority. The South Africa Act is to us, the dispossessed people, what the 1917 Balfour Declaration is to the Palestinian people.

It was in recognition of this national dispossession that Bambata the hero of the 1906 war of resistance said, 'The African people lost their land on the battlefield. They can only regain it in the battlefield.'

References:
1. *The Revolutionary Worker*, 2 October 1981, Chicago, Illinois.
2. ANC (Nationalist), *In Defence of the African Heritage*, Dar-Es-Salaam.
3. *The Sunday Express*, Johannesburg, 14 February 1982.
4. *The Star*, 3 June 1982.
5. *Natal Daily News*, 17 June 1982.
6. From Short Notes supplied by A.P. Mda.
7. Martin J. Murray, *South African Capitalism and Black Political Opposition (1982)*, p.676. Schenkman Publishing Company Inc., Cambridge, Massachusetts.

Appendices

Some important events occurred in Azania after this book was completed. I want to include them because they are indeed very significant for Azania and the freedom-loving people of the world who desire to see Azania liberated.

UDF and National Forum Committee Repeat History

In May 1983 the 'multi-racial' United Democratic Front was formed by 32 organizations at a meeting in Johannesburg. The following month on 12 June the Black-Consciousness oriented National Forum Committee was formed by 200 organizations of the oppressed at Hammanskraal near Pretoria with 800 delegates. On August 20 the United Democratic Front held its first congress near Capetown with 600 delegates attending.

Both the National Forum Committee and the United Democratic Front were formed to oppose the racist regime's constitutional proposals. The settler regime will hold a referendum before the end of this year to create a three-chamber parliament in which the minority whites, the Indians and the Coloureds will be represented. The white Parliament as usual will exclude Africans who constitute 75% of the population and are indigenous to the Azanian soil.

What do the United Democratic Front and the National Forum Committee stand for? And what is their origin and their composition.

The United Democratic Front has been given wide publicity by the Western press and its commentators. The UDF has been described variously as 'multi-racial' 'moderate grouping' willing to co-operate with 'white progressives' and 'democrats'. The UDF membership therefore, consists of people from the oppressed section of the Azanian community and from people in the oppressors' ranks who are 'sympathetic' to the oppression of the Black people, but are themselves living a life as comfortable as that of their oppressor brothers and sisters.

On the other hand the National Forum Committee is composed of only those who are from the oppressed section—the Black people. And this section constitutes 87% of the South African population.

What guides the United Democratic Front and the National Forum Committee?

The origins of the UDF go back to January 1983 when the Rev Allan Boesak, president of the World Alliance of Reformed churches appealed to people of all races in South Africa to form a united front to oppose Botha's Government constitutional proposals. The Rev Boesak is himself a liberal. This being the case, the UDF takes its politics from the controversial document euphemistically called 'Freedom' Charter by its proponents and or adherents. This charter was adopted by what was called the 'Congress Alliance' in Kliptown in 1955.

The charter led to the split in the African National Congress. The 'moderate' wing went along with the Freedom Charter while the militant wing rejected the charter as a 'colossal fraud' and formed the Pan Africanist Congress. The Freedom Charter has its origin in the white middle class of South Africa. The charter proclaims that 'South Africa belongs to all who live in it...'—coloniser and colonised. This annoyed the militant elements who saw this as a falsefication of the country's history and an attempt to interpret the history of Azania in favour of the racist minority who came from Europe to the country as settlers.

In a nutshell those who formed the UDF and call themselves 'progressive democrats' believe that the whites are an integral part of the black struggle. Those in the National Forum Committee hold a contrary view. They believe that whites have no role to play, other than conditioning their fellow whites for the inevitability of black majority rule. This division has led to the National Forum Committee being branded 'racialists' by their detractors, while in turn the pro-NFC elements accuse the so-called 'progressive democrats' of putting whites before blacks.

A leading member of the Black Sash, Sheena Duncan a rather unusual South African white liberal has made an interesting observation. She has said, 'We are aware right now that there are severe divisions between the black consciousness groups and the so-called 'progressive democrats' on the acceptance of whites. We do not see the need for making an issue of ourselves. It is more important that there is solidarity within the black community before we are considered.'

Asked by the *Natal Witness* whether she agreed that whites have not got much of a role to play in the black struggle outside of their community, Mrs Sheena Duncan said, 'The fact is, as Helen Suzman pointed out earlier whites cannot effectively bring about change in this country other than parliamentary opposition. There is no extra-parliamentary option open to us. Taking this into account, I see no point in the 'progressive democrats' making an issue of us. Some of them are my friends, but I think they must realise that right now, black solidarity is more important than white sympathy.'

Some liberals styling themselves as 'progressive democrats' have tried to twist Marxism in Azania in order to confuse the Azanian National struggle. They speak of a 'class struggle'. But they refuse to recognise that the Africans in South Africa belong to the 'have not' class while the whites belong to the 'have' class and enjoy the benefits of the Blackman's oppression. These 'haves' who happen to be white in the South African situation are the perpetrators of the capitalist system. The obvious outcome here is that the 'have nots' stand against the 'haves'—hence the conflict between the whites and the Blacks. Some people think it is rather ironic that the 'progressives' and the 'democrats' are found more in the company of the 'haves'. Some have hurled insults at the organizations of the 'have nots' such as the case when Zinzi Mandela of the United Democratic Front called the leaders of the National Forum Committee 'political bandits'.

The National Forum Committee has rejected the Freedom Charter and has adopted *The Azanian People's Manifesto*. This manifesto states categorically that the Azanian struggle being waged by the toiling masses is nationalist in character and socialist in content. The Black Working Class is the vanguard for this struggle. The Azanian People's Manifesto also makes it clear that the land—Azania belongs to the Azanian people.

The former President of the Azanian Peoples Organisation, Kehla Mthembu (who is now closely connected with the National Forum Committee) warned the Azanian people and said, 'In order for our liberation goal to be meaningful, we must guard against all kinds of watering down our militancy. Change and liberation shall not come as a result of suicidal alliances.... Peace, stability can only be brought by those who know what it is to sleep on an empty stomach, those whose husbands and brothers have died in jail and those who experience oppression practically.'

In actual fact, the UDF and the NFC are a reflection of the African traditional politics within South Africa since 1955 when the whites in the 'Congress Alliance' succeedeed in pushing the ANC to adopt the controversial Freedom Charter.

The adoption of the Freedom Charter resulted in a great deal of polemics and name-calling. The South African liberal press called the chartetists 'moderates' and anti-Freedom Charter elements (the Africanists) 'extremist', 'radical' or 'racialists'.

What is interesting is that many issues which are being discussed today in South Africa about the Azanian struggle for national and social emancipation, were answered by none other than the sublime Mangaliso Sobukwe, Founder-President of the Pan Africanist Congress.

In an interview with *The Africanist* in January 1959, Sobukwe was asked: What are your differences with the ANC?

He answered: First of all we differ radically in our conception of the struggle. We firmly hold that we are oppressed as a subject nation—the African nation. To us, therefore, the struggle is a national struggle. Those of the ANC who are its active policy-makers, maintain, that ours is a class struggle. We are according to them oppressed as workers, both white and black. But it is interesting that they make no attempt whatsoever to organise white workers. Their allies are all of them bourgeois!

Secondly, we differ in our attitude to 'co-operation' with other national groups. Perhaps it might be better to say we differ with them in our understanding of the term 'co-operation'. We believe that co-operation is possible only between equals. There can be no co-operation between oppressor and oppressed, dominating and dominated. That is *collaboration*, not co-operation. And we cannot co-operate in our own oppression! The ANC leadership on the other hand, would seem to regard collaboration and co-operation as synonymous. They seem to believe that all that is required for people to be 'equals' is that they should declare that they are equals, and lo! the trick is done...'

Sobukwe went on to say that the Black people under his leadership stood for 'the complete overthrow of white domination. That means that the South African Act of 1909—that fossilised relic of the whiteman's exclusive privileges and prejudices—must be scrapped.'

Another question which is being asked about Black organisations was also answered by Sobukwe. The question was: What is your answer to the accusation that you are anti-white?

Sobukwe answered: 'To say that we are prepared to accept anybody who subscribes to our programme is but to state a condition that one knows cannot be fulfilled. From past history, not only of this country, but of other countries as well, we know that a group in a privileged position never voluntarily relinquished that position. If some members of the group appear to be sympathetic to the demands of the less privileged, it is only in so far as those demands do not threaten the privileges of the favoured group. If they (the privileged) offer assistance, it is for the purpose of "directing" and "controlling" the struggle of the under-privileged so that it does not become "dangerous" '.

It is important for people who easily get confused about the situation in Azania to note the following point. Before independence in Zimbabwe ZANU PF did not have white members. But that did not make ZANU PF a 'racist' organization. In fact, throughout Africa the majority of political parties did not have white members *before uhuru*. There is nothing virtuous about white membership. PLO as far as is known has no Jewish members. But that does not make PLO anti-Jewish. The reality is that the time for Jews to join the PLO is not ripe. No one has as yet made an issue of the fact that SWAPO has or has not white members. Absence of white membership in a liberation organization is no proof of 'racialism' as 'multi-racialists' often assume. The accusation will be well deserved when Azania is free and truly independent and certain people are refused membership of their political choice on the grounds of their colour or race.

Since it is important for freedom lovers the world over to appreciate the issues that are involved in the Azanian situation as reflected in the National Forum Committee and the United Democratic Front it is proper to quote Sobukwe again because he dealt with these issues clearly a long time ago. He said: 'We stand for equal rights for all individuals. But the whites have to accept allegiance to Africa *first*; once a truly non-racial democracy exists in Azania, all individuals, whatever their colour or race, will be accepted as Africans. *Naturally, we cannot put the cart before the horse*. We have to realise that at the moment the struggle is between a white minority and the oppressed black majority.'

In the Azanian struggle therefore, there are no 'racialists'! Only 'multi-racialists' as seen in the United Democratic Front and 'non-racialists' as represented by the National Forum Committee. The 'multi-racialists' are opening the doors to white membership now. While the 'non-racialists' will open their doors to white membership when freedom is attained in Azania and the primary contradiction which arose when Azania was colonised in 1652 is resolved.

The Azanian People's Manifesto

The historic conference of organizations of the oppressed and exploited people of Azania held at Hammanskraal on 11-12 June 1983 and convened by the National Forum Committee, having deliberated on vital questions affecting Azania resolved to condemn the murder of freedom fighters by the racist minority regime and to issue the following manifesto for consideration by all the organizations of the people to be reviewed at the second National Forum to be convened during the Easter Weekend of 1984.

Manifesto of the Azanian People

Our struggle for national liberation is directed against the system of racial capitalism which holds the people of Azania in bondage for the benefit of the small minority of white capitalists and their allies, the white workers and the reactionary sections of the black middle class. The struggle against apartheid is no more than the point of departure for our liberation efforts. Apartheid will be eradicated with the system of racial capitalism.

The black working class inspired by revolutionary consciousness is the driving force of the struggle. They alone can end the system as it stands today because they alone have nothing at all to loose. They have a world to gain in a democratic, anti-racist and socialist Azania. It is the historic task of the black working class and its organization to mobilise the urban and the rural poor together with the radical sections of the middle classes in order to put an end to the system of oppression and exploitation by the white ruling class.

The successful conduct of national liberation struggle depends on the firm basis of principles whereby we will ensure that liberation will not be turned against our people by treacherous and opportunistic 'leaders'. Of these principles, the most important are:

- Anti-racism and anti-imperialism.
- Non-collaboration with the oppressor and its political instruments.
- Independent working-class organization.
- Opposition to all alliances with ruling-class parties.

In accordance with these principles, the oppressed and exploited people of Azania demand immediately:

- The right to work.
- The right to form trade unions that will heighten revolutionary worker consciousness.
- The establishment of a democratic, anti-racist worker Republic in Azania where the interests of the workers shall be paramount through worker control of the means of production distribution and exchange.
- State provision of free and compulsory education for all and this education be geared towards liberating the Azanian people from all forms of oppression, exploitation and ignorance.
- State provision of adequate and decent housing.
- State provision of free health, legal, recreational and other community services that will respond positively to the needs of the people.
- Development of one national progressive culture in the process of struggle.
- The land and all that belongs to it shall be wholly owned and controlled by the Azanian people.
- The usage of the land and all that accrues to it shall be aimed at ending all forms and means of exploitation.

In order to bring into effect these demands of the Azanian people, we pledge ourselves to struggle tirelessly for:

- The abolition of all laws that discriminate against our people on the basis of colour, sex, religion or language.
- The abolition of all influx control measures and pass laws.
- The abolition of all resettlement and group areas removals.
- Reintegration of the bantustan human dumping grounds into a unitary Azania.

Resolutions of the National Forum Committee

Resolution 1: That this house express its condolences to the next-of-kin of the three freedom fighters murdered on Thursday by the racist Botha regime.
Resolution 2: That this National Forum noting:

1. The struggle waged by the toiling masses is nationalist in character and socialist in content.
2. The Black working class is the vanguard of this just struggle towards the total liberation from racist capitalism.
3. The future of Azanian state will be an anti-racist, democratic one.
4. The international imperialism and racist capitalism systems promote the bantustans as counter-revolutionary elements to the revolutionary forces.

And further noting that
The usage of the land shall not be to the benefit of Azanians only but for the benefit of all Africa...

Therefore resolves that:

1. The land and all that belongs to it will be wholly owned and controlled by the Azanian people.
2. Each individual will be expected to contribute labour according to ability.
3. All the proceeds accruing to collective labour shall be distributed according to the needs of each and every individual in Azania.
4. The usage of the land and all that accrues to it shall be aimed at ending all forms of exploitation of man by man.

Resolution 3: Seeing that relevant and reliable communication between the oppressed masses is minimal and does not fully express their aspirations, because we have to contend with the white liberal press, state-controlled radio and television and literature expressing a ruling class perspective and also serving to propagate the apartheid ideology.

And seeing that the present means of communication only reaches literate people.

We resolve that:

1. Cultural organizations be fully supported and utilised to enhance communication amongst the people by forming units that would take relevant art and literature, especially drama as it uses the spoken word.

Resolution 4: That this house declares its non-recognition and rejection of any portion of the Azanian soil being alienated.

We also declare that the Azanian People's Republic will demand back such portion of land with all the power at its command.

And this house further supports the legitimate right of the Namibian people to the area called Walvis Bay as being their property and not belonging to the racist South African regime.

Resolution 5: That this house assures the colonially oppressed people of Namibia that the Azanian people are unalterably opposed to the colonial war being waged by the South African Aggressive Forces against the people of Namibia. We call on the racist forces to be withdrawn forthwith from Namibia and from any neighbouring African state.

We call on the illegal regime to allow the people of Namibia their right to self-determination.

And further, we condemn all military and political interference by the South African Aggressive Forces in the affairs of any African State.

Index

192 *Index*